CONTENTS

PREFACE

Wake up, and strengthen the things that remain, which were about to die; for I have not found your deeds completed in the sight of My God. So, remember what you have received and heard; and keep it, and repent. Therefore, if you do not wake up, I will come like a thief, and you will not know at what hour I will come to you.

Revelation 3:2

G.K. Chesterton once said, "An open mind is like an open mouth. Both are meant to close on something." Our kids come into this world both physically and spiritually vulnerable. Because of this natural vulnerability, parents must carefully attend both the physical and spiritual needs of their children. The Christian worldview demands we not only feed them bread at the supper table but also a steady dose of the "living bread that came down from heaven" (Jn. 6:51). Our children's minds will "close on something" whether we like it or not. The "something" will shape the way they view God, themselves, the world, and their purpose in it. No one is a greater mover in shaping the "something" than the parents.

It is my hope that the following pages encourage parents to take a hard look at the details of their current home life. The choices we make in discipline, sports, family worship, spiritual disciplines, internet protection, and sharing the gospel — along with a thousand other daily things — have a profound effect on our children.

Jesus says in Luke 6:40, "A pupil is not above his teacher; but everyone, after he has been fully trained, will be like his teacher." Parents are teaching their kids life priorities 24/7. This should give us parents pause and cause us to carefully evaluate what we teach and how we teach it. Parents need to abdicate less and take more responsibility in the spiritual shaping of their children. It may mean giving up a hobby or two. It may mean choosing one sport at a time for your child, instead of two or three. These daily choices we make not only shape our children now but also influence their future choices as parents.

Revelation 3:2 was originally written for the church of Sardis. Like so many of us, they were distracted by things of no eternal value. Because of this, they were warned to "strengthen the things that remain." C.S. Lewis said in *The Four Loves*, "all that is not eternal is eternally out of date." We should parent with a spiritual end in mind, an eternal perspective. This means we must constantly reevaluate our priorities and decisions from year to year. One day your child will leave the home. Don't let that time sneak up on you. Sow things of eternal value into their lives and into yours. Think, "What will my legacy be when I pass from this life?"

Parents have approached me more times than I can count, struggling with how to counsel their children who've asked about becoming a Christian. I've also counseled parents who wonder when their children might be ready for baptism. Marriage and sex are also critical topics parents may not know how to approach. They must be proactive when addressing all these subjects, and they must do so with a biblical worldview. This book seeks to meet these needs, helping parents discuss important topics with their children before the outside world does it for them.

But, there are other things Christian parents must consider. Not only must they answer their children's questions, but they must also create an environment conducive for their children to grow as believers. This includes fostering reverence for God in our homes. I have included some ideas for family worship as well as other resources to encourage faithful growth in this area.

While each chapter's topic(s) could be a book in and of itself, I have sought to cover multiple topics relevant to parents today in one small work. The advice for parents in this book ranges from suggested readings for three-year-olds all the way to apologetics for college kids. It is my prayer that God will work through these words by the power of the Holy Spirit and bless each of your families in every way.

May His Kingdom come on earth as it is in Heaven!

Martin Winslow

CHAPTER ONE

GOSPEL ESSENTIALS AND BAPTISM

"The greatest need in the world today is the gospel. It is the greatest need of the world because men, women, and children are perishing without a vital knowledge of God through the good news of our Savior and his Son, Jesus."
Thabiti M. Anyabwile[1]

"For I delivered to you as of first importance what I also received, that Christ died for our sins according to the Scriptures, and that He was buried, and that He was raised on the third day according to the Scriptures…"
I Corinthians 15:3-4

MY TWO PAULS

THE APOSTLE PAUL BEGAN HIS LETTER TO THE GALATIANS BY telling them that accepting any gospel other than the one he had preached to them was to accept a false one. He went on to say that if they accepted another so-called gospel, they would be under the curse of God (Anathema). The word *gospel* means "good news." You and I need this good news because we were born into this world with very bad news; we are born spiritually dead (Eph. 2:1-3) and without spiritual eyes to discern (1 Cor. 2:14). We are not just indifferent to God, but as C. S. Lewis put it, "rebels who need to lay down our arms."[2]

Our gospel presentation to our children consists of more than what we teach them from Scripture. It includes how we live out our lives in front of them and how we interact with them. The apostle Paul lived what he preached. Your child's understanding of grace, faith, repentance, and forgiveness will be shaped mostly by you, but the Christians around them who teach them the Word will also have a part to play. Paul's biblical writings helped me understand my sinfulness and separation from God (2 Cor. 5:21). He also wrote about what it means to love like Jesus (2 Cor. 9:22). Both his words and the way he lived his life continue to influence the Church through Scripture.

THE BAD NEWS: I MUST GIVE AN ACCOUNT

I remember the "bad news" as it was articulated to me by one of the kindest men I've ever met. It was another Paul — Paul Benne. He understood the apostle Paul's gospel. When Benne spoke of spiritual things, he made me feel as though I'd been punched in the face and hugged at the same time. He was grace and truth all at once — a rare gift.

I was nine years old, attending Paul's Sunday school classroom at the little Nazarene church in Esther, Missouri. Paul was a gentle, kind, and loving man, and he loved our little classroom full of wild boys. Each week, he brought us Star-Crunch, Oatmeal Crème Pies, donuts, and chocolate milk. Paul patiently taught and disciplined us. Instead of making us listen and be good first, he gave us snacks at the start of class. Now, as I reflect on how vivid my memories are of that class, I wonder if all that sugar heightened our senses. Maybe that was his plan all along!

On this particular day, as I was halfway through my second Star-Crunch and bouncing off the walls, he began to teach. He was undeterred as always. Paul talked about that "bad news." He told me I was accountable before God for my sins, that unless Jesus paid for my sins, I was going to have to pay for them myself. This got my attention. I was old enough to know I had already committed plenty of sins. St. Augustine said when he saw the truth of the gospel but still wanted to live in the world, he would pray, "Lord make me chaste, but not yet."[3] I was in that stage of life. I didn't want to pay for my sins, but I also didn't want to do things God's way. I could already understand the gospel intellectually as being the "good news" I needed, but I still wasn't born again. God used Paul's words that day as a piece of the gospel puzzle for me.

Think of your children's spiritual journey like a puzzle for them to solve. Like my Sunday school teacher, you can give your children pieces of that same puzzle. Picture discipling them as the process of guiding them as they put together a puzzle you've already completed. When you look at the pieces in a pile, all scattered and disarrayed, you can clearly see where they should go. Because of this, if you aren't careful, you can get annoyed, even impatient, as your child puts together the puzzle. You have to remember that God placed you in your child's life to assist them as they piece together their own spiritual puzzle of reconciliation to God. They aren't born understanding their condition. You are the guide who helps them make sense of the world, but you are only the guide. Ultimately, it is their puzzle. You want them to put it together correctly so they have a thriving relationship with the Lord. Being a part of this process requires patience and commitment. As a child fits the pieces together one at a time, he moves closer to that moment of conversion where things finally fall into place.

FAITH AND GRACE

As you teach your children, it's important to remember that becoming a Christian is more than assenting to a number of propositions. It is perfectly possible to have a child who is not a Christian but believes, intellectually, that Jesus died on a cross for the sins of the world and that a person can go to heaven. They can walk forward during a church service, be baptized, and participate in the Lord's Supper, all while lacking true faith.

James says, "... demons believe [intellectually] and shudder" (James 2:19). Following Jesus is more than believing an intellectual list of propositions. Faith includes intellectual assent but goes beyond that to trust in Jesus and action resulting from a changed heart. John Calvin once said "It is therefore faith alone which justifies, and yet the faith which justifies is not alone."[4] Saving faith is active faith. It is compelled past propositions to action. A follower of Jesus is in active pursuit of him. That's not to say true Christians don't stumble; they certainly do. The difference is that the true believer does not give up. He continues to press on and pursue his Master. Jesus said in John 10:4, "When he puts forth all his own, he goes ahead of them, and the sheep follow him because they know his voice." 1 John 1:6-7 says, "If we say that we have fellowship with him and yet walk in the darkness, we lie and do not practice the truth. But if we walk in the Light as he himself is in the Light, we have fellowship with one another, and the blood of Jesus his Son cleanses us from all sin."

I am not saying good works save us. They do not. Works are the outgrowth of legitimate faith in the gospel. Ephesians 2:8-10 says, "For by grace you have been saved through faith, and that not of yourselves; it is the gift of God, not as a result of works, so that no one may boast. For we are his workmanship, created in Christ Jesus for good works, which God prepared beforehand so that we would walk in them." Grace saves us. This is the unmerited favor of God. No one deserves it, yet it is freely given. Receiving something deserved is akin to receiving something owed; this is not grace. God's grace is expressed in his free offer of salvation. Man's faith in Christ's redemptive work is the vehicle which drives us to accept that grace.

How can you teach these concepts of grace and faith to your children?

I suggest giving them simple lessons on grace and faith. Take your child on a random trip for ice cream. When they ask the occasion, tell them it isn't because of anything they have done. In fact, you can point out reasons they don't deserve it. Tell them that because you love them, even when they don't deserve it, you are compelled to do good things for them. Then, talk about Romans 5:6, which says, "For while we were still helpless, at the right time Christ died for the ungodly."

I also like the object lesson of the "trust fall" to illustrate faith to children. Simply stand behind them, having them stand stiff as a board with their eyes closed or blindfolded. Count to three and have them fall. Make sure to catch them! This is way harder than you might think if you have never seen it done before. This kind of faith forces your children to learn they must trust you even when they cannot see what the outcome will be. It also teaches them that genuine faith requires risk on their part (Heb. 11). True faith believes, trusts, and does something about it. The trust fall is a scary moment that requires willful action for the one falling. It isn't enough to believe you will be caught. You must follow through by falling. James 2:18 says, "But someone may well say, you have faith and I have works; show me your faith without works, and I will show you my faith by my works." James and the Apostle Paul are not at odds. Read in their proper contexts, they complement each other just as God the Holy Spirit intended.

Our children should realize that the Christian has been set apart from the world by the faith we have placed in the grace of Christ. Help them understand that the world watches those who claim to have received God's life-changing grace. As the world watches us, there should exist a drastic difference in the way we conduct our lives as new creations. It should awe the impatient world to see us wait patiently. It should shock them to see our quiet, gentle answer turn away wrath. It should blow their mind when we strive to be peacemakers in the midst of a dog-eat-dog world!

We won't always make perfect decisions, but grace will always be extended to us. Grace functions for us like a safety net. We are not to take advantage of it, but it's there for us flawed yet redeemed children of Adam. Make no mistake; biblical faith gravitates toward Jesus, not away from him. We mess up, but as believers, we find our way back to the oasis of hope.

Christians typically stress the dates and times we decided to become a Christian, but the Christian life is more than looking back to a time when something happened. Something should be happening in your life now. God is real, alive, and active in you right now if you are his child (John 14:7). You don't need to invite him into your home; he is already there. You don't need to invite him into the workplace or your Monday morning coffee meeting with friends. He is present. God does not stay in the sanctuary of your church on Sunday morning when the service is over. God is very present with us, and we should be pursuing his voice more and more each day. Your children must know that followers of Jesus are to be in constant pursuit of him. In fact, the word *pursuit* is built into our original name.

DISCIPLES/FOLLOWERS OF THE WAY

The word *Christian* is used only three times in the New Testament — Acts 11:26, Acts 26:28, and 1 Peter 4:16[5] — and it's used in a negative way. It was coined by unbelievers and meant to belittle the believer.[6]

But, how did the early church describe itself? The word *disciple*, which comes from the Greek word *mathetes* and literally means "student" or "disciple,"[7] is used 261 times in the Gospels and the book of Acts.[8] Now, think of the difference between asking if someone is a Christian and asking them if they are a disciple of Jesus. The word *disciple* implies a life of study, a life of learning. Jesus tells his disciples in the Great Commission to go and make more disciples. He goes on to say, "[teach] them to observe all that I have commanded you" (Matt. 28:20). Being a disciple of Jesus is a life-long journey of learning and growing.

Christians also described themselves in the New Testament as "the Way," most likely stemming from Jesus' famous statement, "I am the Way" (John 14:6). This implies movement and direction. Paul says, "I admit that I worship the God of our ancestors as a follower of the Way, which they call a sect" (Acts 24:14). Other passages that refer to early Christians as "the Way" include Acts 9:2; 19:9, 23; 22:4; and 24:14, 22.

Think of Christians as travelers on the road to Jesus. We hear his voice; we follow him. The Church follows the Way and shows the Way by proclaiming the gospel to the world. We should encourage our children and remind ourselves that to be a disciple is to be in pursuit of Jesus. We follow his lead and are always committed students of Scripture.

In Luke 6:40, Jesus says something frightening: "A student is not above his teacher, but when he has been fully trained, he will be like him." Parents, you are the primary teachers of your children. You may give others some authority, but you are mainly responsible. Jesus' message is imperative. Our children will learn from us, and they will *be like us*. Have you ever thought, "I just sounded like my mom or dad?" Then, Jesus' words have rung true in your life. It will be the same with your own children. What are their teachers like? Are your kids following you as you follow Christ, or are you making it up as you go? Be a disciple. Be a "follower of the Way."

JUSTIFICATION: CAPTAIN AMERICA'S SHIELD... OUTSIDE PROTECTION

No one is perfect, even Christians. You might realize this, but has your child? They may believe that attending church, obeying their parents, and generally being a good person will somehow make them right before God. Not so! The biblical teaching is that Christians have a foreign righteousness that is not their own that has been credited to their account.

Let me break that down a little. The Reformed view of justification is that an exchange occurred at the cross. Jesus suffered the consequences of the sin debt we owed to a holy God. He became our substitute. The wrath we deserved was poured out upon him, leading to our forgiveness. But that is only half of justification. We not only received forgiveness but also the imputed righteousness of Christ. The perfect righteousness of Jesus was credited to our account at the cross.

I didn't suddenly become righteous when I believed the gospel. Instead, the righteousness of Jesus was appropriated to me. Luther said the redeemed believer is "fully just and fully sinful at the same time."[9] I explain it to my kids this way: if I were going to be attacked, and Captain America threw me his shield to protect myself, his shield didn't suddenly become my shield. I am borrowing his shield, and because I have it, I am protected from Red Skull or whoever else I am fighting. God the Father who is the Righteous Judge acquits us based not on our merits but those of Christ; we only borrow them.

God's justification of us based on the work of Christ is considered outside of us. We don't magically become inwardly righteous because of justification. Instead, we become outwardly protected from the wrath of God we deserve. Jesus took that wrath on the cross and saved us from it, but God also credits the Son's righteousness to our account. Verse four of the famous song "My Hope is Built on Nothing Less" says:

> When He shall come with trumpet sound,
> Oh, may I then in him be found;
> In him, my righteousness, alone,
> faultless to stand before the throne.[10]

Isn't this amazing news for the Christian? This whole song might be one that you consider singing with your family. If you do, use the song as a catalyst to explain justification to your children.

The Gospel Coalition has a great statement on the justification of sinners:

> We believe that Christ, by his obedience and death, fully discharged the debt of all those who are justified. By his sacrifice, he bore in our stead the punishment due us for our sins, making a proper, real, and full satisfaction to God's justice on our behalf. By his perfect obedience he satisfied the just demands of God on our behalf, since by faith alone that perfect obedience is credited to all who trust in Christ alone for their acceptance with God. Inasmuch

as Christ was given by the Father for us, and his obedience and punishment were accepted in place of our own, freely and not for anything in us, this justification is solely of free grace, in order that both the exact justice and the rich grace of God might be glorified in the justification of sinners. We believe that a zeal for personal and public obedience flows from this free justification.[11]

SANCTIFICATION: POPEYE'S SPINACH... CHANGES INSIDE WHICH AFFECT THE OUTSIDE

When someone believes the gospel, he is not only justified and protected because of the work of Christ but also made new on the inside. We call this being born again (John 3) or regeneration. When regeneration takes place, the process of sanctification begins inside the believer. This is a lifelong process of growing in Christ. While justification means we are instantly pardoned of sin, sanctification means we begin the marathon of the Christian life. As God through his Holy Spirit reveals sin, we repent and continue to believe the gospel. Through sanctification, the will of God becomes important to us. Whereas before we only thought of the things we wanted, we now begin to love the things God loves. We also have a deeper understanding and recognition of our own personal sin. Our weaknesses become clearer and so does God's holiness. The Second London Baptist Confession says regarding sanctification, "This sanctification is throughout the whole man, yet imperfect in this life; there abideth still some remnants of corruption in every part, whence ariseth a continual and irreconcilable war; the flesh lusting against the Spirit, and the Spirit against the flesh."[12]

When I was a child, I used to watch the cartoon *Popeye*. He would eat his spinach so he could whip Brutus. He tilted his head, opened his mouth wide, dumped in the entire can, and swallowed. The spinach caused an outside physical change. His muscles bulged, and his appearance actually transformed. I tell my kids that sanctification is the spiritual nourishment we need on the inside. When we walk by God's Spirit in sanctification, it comes out in our actions. Our spiritual muscles grow. We are able to whip the enemy by making decisions in line with the will of Christ. I might be a bit outdated, but show your kids a YouTube video of Popeye eating his spinach, just for me, okay?

REPENTANCE

Sharing the gospel in the home is much like how Paul Benne shared it with me. God uses little pieces of truth over time to bring your child to a conviction of sin and a desperate need to be reconciled to him. The apostle Paul tells us we are "ministers of reconciliation" (2 Cor. 5:18).

Be careful in how you speak to your children. When you spend too much time talking about being saved or missing out on heaven, you put the emphasis on their making a decision to merely benefit themselves. While those things may be true, it's important to stress the need for relationship with God. Our sin offends our Creator, and we need reconciliation between us and God. Stressing relationship implies something ongoing. It moves past the mere decision stage of Christianity and helps children realize that faith is not just believing certain things but pursuing God.

Paul says, "Now all these things are from God, who reconciled us to himself through Christ and gave us the ministry of reconciliation, namely, that God was in Christ reconciling the world to himself, not counting their trespasses against them, and he has committed to us the word of reconciliation" (2 Cor. 5:18-19). Repentance is an ongoing reconciliation with God that the Christian must continually seek. Sin breaks relationship; repentance repairs it.

We usually think of John the Baptist as preaching repentance, but Jesus did as well. In Mark 1:15, we see the first glimpse of Jesus preaching: "The time is fulfilled, and the kingdom of God is at hand; repent and believe the gospel." For years, passages like Mark 1:15 were misunderstood. It was thought during the Middle Ages that a person had to carry out an act of penance to negate a committed sin. In other words, the person was given a prescription of action by the priest to help in the forgiveness process. This key misunderstanding to the gospel on the part of the Catholic Church is what so enraged Luther during the Reformation.

Because the Holy Spirit lives in believers, we can turn from sin. When we were born again, we received power from God. When sin creeps up on us, we should turn in earnestness to "walk in the light as he is in the light" (1 John 1:7). When we fail, we fall into the net of grace, but we quickly take responsibility and march back toward God. R. C. Sproul in his book, *Chosen by God*, gives the following chart to demonstrate man's ability to choose through the ages.[13]

Pre-Fall Man	Post-Fall Man	Reborn Man	Glorified Man
Able to sin	Able to sin	Able to sin	
Able to not sin		Able to not sin	Able to not sin
	Unable to not sin		
			Unable to sin

Notice the "reborn man" has the ability through the power of God to choose what is right. He has been liberated through the power of Jesus from the power of original sin. In speaking with your child, always stress the importance of their relationship with God. We are made for a relationship with Jesus, and this is why repentance is so beautiful. It demonstrates our willingness through God's power to choose what is good.

In his great work, *The Doctrine of Repentance*, Thomas Watson tells the story of a pastor who asked three different men why they chose to leave sin and follow Jesus. One says, "I think of the joys of heaven." Another says, "I think of the torments of hell," but the third replied, "I think of the love of God, and that makes me forsake it

[sin]. How shall I offend the God of love?"[14] The first two persons approached God with their own interests in mind. The third approached God with relationship in mind. Typically, we say repentance means to turn from sin, and this is true. The Greek word *metanoia* means "a change of mind, turning about, or conversion."[15]

But there is more to the process, and Watson breaks it down nicely. I would challenge you to examine the following steps of repentance carefully in the life of your child and explain each stage:

1. A person must see sin in order to turn from it.
2. A person must feel the grief of sin before he is truly sorry.
3. A person must overcome pride and take responsibility for sin.
4. A person must feel the brokenness of relationship with God and others.
5. A person must learn to hate what God hates.
6. This necessary process leads to true repentance.[16]

REPENTANCE AND RELATIONSHIP

Your personal relationships will be defined on a practical level by your ability to repent of sin when confronted. Parents, it starts with you. You and I must take responsibility for our failures so our children learn how to take responsibility for theirs. Children are always watching us. When we repent, we both accept that the law is good (1 Tim. 1:8) and that we are in need of grace. If we can't deal with our weaknesses and failures and take responsibility for them, then we must prepare for a life of fake relationships. We will never crack the surface of a true relationship if we can't own up to our own failures, receive grace, and allow our friends to do the same. Our children will most likely follow in our footsteps.

If our pride keeps us from repentance with those closest to us, whether family or friends, we must do some serious soul searching. "God is opposed to the proud, but gives grace to the humble"

(James 4:6). I've noticed that prideful people love it when someone takes responsibility for a wrong committed against them, but they also sparingly give grace. They enjoy seeing others come groveling for forgiveness. This is not the Spirit of Christ, but the antithesis. What are they modeling to their children? Certainly not Christlikeness. At the height of pain and suffering, Jesus said, "Father forgive them" (Luke 23:34). Real relationships are a struggle. We must be willing to own up to our failures and live in the life-giving power of Christ's forgiveness, then be willing to extend it to others.

Parents must understand that their children are watching. As parents, we will make plenty of mistakes. We will sin against others, including our own children. When we realize it, we must model a humble and repentant heart. We must teach our children that we are humble enough to confess and repent of our sins, and at the same time, we must humbly receive their confessions and repentance with forgiveness.

DON'T "SAVE" YOUR CHILDREN FROM REPENTANCE

The worst thing you can do for your children if they are caught in sin is to defend them and get them off the hook. Parents raising their kids in a no-consequence world will watch them pay for it when they are older.

Once, after we ordered our kids water to drink at Dairy Queen, I noticed them all getting refills before we left. When we got home, I saw that one of my children had filled her cup with fruit punch. Dairy Queen was five miles away, and it was late. I talked with my daughter, and clearly she knew she had done wrong. What was I to do: issue a stern warning and let it go or drive back into town and make it right? It's just fruit punch! Dairy Queen wouldn't know! She's a kid, right? Wrong. It was clear to me that she needed to confess the sin and repent of it. I told her to get her piggy bank. We were going to Dairy Queen to meet with the manager on duty. She was stressed, but in my mind, it was a lot better to address it at eight years old rather than sixteen, after her character (or lack thereof) was already developed.

On the way back to Dairy Queen that night I never said, "I can't believe you did that!" I didn't berate her. She was in inner turmoil, convicted of her sin. I could see it all over her face. So, I patiently coached her on how to take responsibility when we got there — what she should say, what she should not say, and how to make Jesus happy. We prayed together in the parking lot and then went in. My daughter did great. With tears in her eyes, she explained what she had done and asked the manager to forgive her. The manager graciously told her she didn't have to pay for the juice. I insisted that she did. Our children sometimes need to feel the sting of sin, and we were going to see this teachable moment through.

Remember, it is the law that drives us to our need for the Gospel. These types of lessons are important for our children, and while they aren't a huge deal in big people world, we are helping them grow in Christ. This experience was both embarrassing and liberating for my eight-year-old. She told me on the way home she was glad we returned for her to apologize. She didn't think she would have been able to sleep if we hadn't. My daughter learned that night to walk through confession and repentance and realized that on the other side there was grace. I couldn't have been more proud of her. She, like you and me, was a sinner saved by grace.

BAPTISM AND CHILDREN

When is it right to baptize a child? I hold to the credobaptist position, which is that baptism is for believers only. The reformed tradition views baptism as a sign of the covenant promises of God to believing families, and therefore, they baptize their infant children (paedobaptism). While I have a lot of respect and agree theologically with almost all historic reformed positions, this is one with which I don't agree.

For the last twenty years, I have heard parents who are credobaptists ask the question, "When is my child ready for baptism?" Sometimes a child's friend is baptized, and they want to be as well. Sometimes a child's older sibling has made the decision to follow Christ, and the child wants to be like them. Sometimes children have made some sort of decision at a camp, and it's hard to tell what happened. Maybe they heard the gospel at VBS, and now they want to be baptized. They followed a formula, and now they say they are ready. The parents are anxious, excited that something is going on with their child, and the last thing they want to hear from me is, "I don't think he is ready yet."

I will just say this: only John the Baptist is reported to have been "filled with the Holy Spirit from his mother's womb" (Luke 1:15). Many times parents, thinking baptism seals the salvation deal with God, are quick to want their children baptized when they are too young. I can't tell you how many stories I have heard from Christians telling me they don't think they were actually a believer when they were baptized as kids. Because of this, many have a crisis of conscience later and want to be baptized again as an adult.

To prevent this from happening, slow down and make sure your child has connected with what it means to be a lifelong follower of Jesus. We live in a culture where men and women take vows before God and the world, committing to each other until death, and are divorced within five years. Does a small child really understand the lifelong commitment to follow Jesus? I am not saying God doesn't move little hearts sometimes and some children are able to understand. I am saying when this happens to kids under around seven or eight years old, they are exceptions and not the rules. I like to have the child articulate to me what is actually happening in his heart and mind. If your child isn't ready to have a discussion and articulate that he believes in the sacrificial death, burial, and resurrection that leads to salvation (the heart of the gospel), then he or she isn't ready. You want to make sure that when your child is baptized, he or she is walking with Jesus and committed to following him.

DON'T WORRY IF YOU ARE UNSURE

In time, it will become clear to both you and your child if he or she has been born again. Baptism does not save a soul. Faith in the grace of the gospel saves a person from the wrath to come. Paul says in 1 Corinthians 1:17, "Christ did not send me to baptize, but to preach the Gospel, not in cleverness of speech, so that the cross of Christ would not be void." Notice how Paul clearly delineates between baptism and the gospel. If your child has truly believed in the gospel and become a committed follower of Jesus, then don't sweat waiting a while for baptism. Lead your child in Bible readings and devotionals to grow his newfound faith. Strengthen him with good biblical teaching, and you will both know soon enough if he or she is ready. Also, consult a pastor and close friends who walk with the Lord so you have help in discerning when your child is ready.

The Didache is an early church document that means "teaching of the twelve." It is thought to contain handed-down traditions of the disciples and dates to around AD 96. It suggests that the one being baptized should fast from food for a couple of days prior to the baptism, along with others who might want to fast on their behalf. This is to help fully focus the heart of the one being baptized on their relationship with God. Not a bad idea for teens and adults!

WHAT DOES BAPTISM MEAN?

Maybe you've heard a parent explain baptism by comparing it to a wedding ring. "It isn't my marriage, but it symbolizes my marriage." Maybe they go on to say, "It is made from the most precious metal. It's in a circle to demonstrate that it never ends." In other words, it's a symbol. Or maybe you've heard the illustration that baptism represents being buried with Christ in death (going under the water) and being risen to new life (coming out of the water). Water also represents spiritual cleanliness from sin because of water's cleansing properties. All of these are true statements about baptism. It is a public way of identifying as a follower of Jesus. Whether in a pool, river, or baptistry, baptism is a powerful statement about inward change.

This is one of the problems I have with paedobaptism. A baby cannot profess to follow Jesus and have an inward experience of the gospel. What we see in the early church through the book of Acts are baptisms of professing believers. We also see in the Great Commission a sequential order given by Jesus. "Go therefore and *make disciples* of all the nations, *baptizing them* in the name of the Father and the Son and the Holy Spirit, *teaching them* to observe all that I commanded..." (Matthew 28:18-20, emphasis mine). Notice that first the disciple is made, then the disciple is baptized, and then the disciple is taught. Baptism is step two for new disciples. They have embraced the Christian life to become a follower of Jesus, and the baptism is a significant, powerful, public display of the power of the gospel to bury the old person and raise a new person who has been cleansed with the blood of Jesus.

Make sure when the day comes for your child to be baptized, you make a big deal out of its significance. Celebrate this with family, friends, and the body of Christ.

Now, you may be thinking to yourself, "How in the world will I talk to my child about these huge terms like grace, faith, justification, sanctification, repentance, and baptism?" All I can say is you've got to try. It's not as hard as you might think. There are plenty of resources (some of which I'll mention here in this book) that can help.

Don't underestimate your children. Read an elementary school text book and then try to tell me kids can't learn the great truths of the faith. I simply don't believe it. Experience has taught me otherwise. Psalm 127 tells us our children are "our reward" and they are to be "like arrows in the hand of a mighty warrior." As we prepare them to engage in the spiritual battle all Christians face (Eph. 6), let's sharpen those little arrows so they are ready to build the kingdom of God.

Good questions to ask yourself and your child:

1. Am I a student of Jesus? If so, how? Remember, "disciple" means student!
2. Am I on the road to Jesus? Am I following his Way? Is my life one that shows others the Way?
3. Have I committed to being a lifelong follower of Christ?

Take time to memorize the definitions of these important terms with your child:

Grace: God's unmerited gift to his children.
Faith: Belief that trusts and compels one to action.

The following definitions come from *The Truth and Grace Memory Book 1*:

Justification: It is God regarding sinners as if they had never sinned and granting them righteousness.

Sanctification: It is God making sinners holy in heart and conduct.

Repentance: To be sorry for sin, and to hate and forsake it because it is displeasing to God.[17]

CHAPTER TWO

HOW DO I KEEP CHRIST AT THE CENTER?

Many of us are missing something in life because we are after the second best, I put before you what I have found to be the best — one who is worthy of all our devotion — Jesus Christ. He is the Savior for the young and the old. Lord, here I am...[1]

    Eric Liddell

Hear, O Israel! The Lord is our God, the Lord is one! You shall love the Lord your God with all your heart and with all your soul and with all your might. These words, which I am commanding you today, shall be on your heart. You shall teach them diligently to your sons and shall talk of them when you sit in your house and when you walk by the way and when you lie down and when you rise up. You shall bind them as a sign on your hand and they shall be as frontals on your forehead. You shall write them on the doorposts of your house and on your gates.

    Deuteronomy 6:4-9

YOU MAY BE THINKING, "REALLY? WHEN THEY GET UP IN THE morning, when they go to sleep, and all the time in between? That's a lot of time teaching my kids. What about my work schedule (or volunteer roles, kids' sports, friends, home life, etc.)?" This might feel daunting or even outdated. You're not alone. Activities such as reading the Bible with your family, sitting around the dinner table, praying together, and having personal, meaningful conversations on an ongoing basis are not part of our culture anymore. Many of us are so busy that by the time we get home at night, we feel like collapsing. For a season, this might be justifiable, but if it is standard practice, it may be time for you to consider a hard reset.

CAPTURING THE ESSENCE OF THIS PASSAGE (24/7)

Deuteronomy 6:4-9 is referred to as the *Shema*. The word *shema* means "listen" and is the first word in verse 4. In this passage, Moses recounts all God's expectations to the children of Israel before they enter the land of promise. The title *Deuteronomy* literally means "second law." It is the second time the law is given, and it arrived at a critical time for all future Israelite families. Since the family is the first institution created by God (Gen. 1-2), Moses takes the time to pointedly specify God's words concerning his expectations for parents when they inherit the land of promise.

Moses says first, "Listen!" This Hebrew word is written in the imperative mood, meaning it is a command, and it's placed first to draw attention to what follows. He then reminds the people not to forget there is only one God. Monotheism (the worship of one God) set the Hebrews apart from all other Mesopotamian religions at the time. They were not to get swept away by polytheism (worshiping many gods) when they moved into the new land. Also, since they knew God and were created by him and for him, they were to love him with everything. This knowledge and love needed to come from the innermost being (the heart). Because knowing, loving, and serving the one true God is the most critical thing for all humanity, they were to intentionally pour these truths into future generations.

This shows us the time to teach our children is always. Teaching God's ways must permeate our lives. Many Jewish people today take these passages ultra-literally and strap tefillin (little boxes filled with Scripture) on their foreheads and bodies. They also mount mezuzahs (boxes filled with Scripture) on the outside doorposts of their homes. While these extremes are unnecessary, it is still imperative for believers to take all precautions and diligently pass the faith on to our children. In Joshua's farewell speech to the children of Israel after seizing the land of promise, he offers these last words: "Choose this day whom you will serve, but as for me and my house, we will serve the LORD" (Josh. 24:15). Unfortunately, the Israelites quickly made the decision to ignore both Moses and Joshua and worship idols instead. The entire book of Judges shows the judgment that came upon the tribes of Israel for this disobedience before the kingdom united under Saul.

The bottom line in the above passage is that God has called fathers and mothers to raise their children with a worldview that glorifies him twenty-four-seven. Obviously, we will fall short in this task, but we must give it our all before our children grow up and enter the world where they will be bombarded with ungodly messages. Jesus deserves our best effort. He is worthy of all praise and all honor in our homes. Let's strive for excellence at all times.

You might ask, "At all times? Isn't that a little extreme?"

The apostle Paul didn't think so.

THE PAIDEIA OF GOD

Paul says in Ephesians 6:4, "Fathers, do not provoke your children to anger, but bring them up in the discipline and instruction of the Lord." Douglas Wilson — the pastor of Christ Church in Moscow, Idaho — sheds light on how the original hearers of the Ephesian letter would have understood this passage. The "instruction of the Lord" was not limited to what we may think of as classroom instruction but reached into every area of society. The Greek word for instruction is *paideia*.[2] Wilson says:

> ... formal education is essential to the process of paideia, of course, but the boundaries of paideia are much wider than the boundaries of what we understand as education. So, our helpful Ephesian would tell us that paideia is certainly the word we are

looking for, but he would then think for a moment and go on to tell us that it is not quite that simple. In short, their paideia was broader, bigger, deeper, and far more developed than our notions of what constitutes "education."[3]

In other words, "the instruction of the Lord" is not just educating our kids with more factoids and Bible lessons. The Greek understanding would have been what Wilson calls "enculturation," instructing our kids with truth as it relates to every aspect of culture.[4] This would mean giving our children a biblical worldview of art, language, science, mathematics, human beings, the internet, and everything else under the sun. *Paideia* is parents' devotion to the idea of helping their kids think God's thoughts after him.

It is critical that parents pass on to their children the "discipline and instruction of the Lord." It may be hard work, but fear not; if you have the heart to pass on to your children a living, vibrant, enthusiastic faith, then now is the time to begin taking baby steps toward that goal. How you live, your priorities, the things you invest your time and money into — this is all being recorded on the little hard drives we call children. They see everything you do. They learn their own priorities from watching yours. You are already shaping who they are going to be.

Do you know how I know that? Because we hear our parents in our discipline. We see our frugality or liberality with finances coming from the way we were raised. Our movie preferences, food choices, and a plethora of other personal idiosyncrasies can be traced back to that little herd you ran with years ago between the ages of one and eighteen. Was the instruction of God recorded on your hard drive during your upbringing? What is being recorded by your children? Is it the instruction of God, or is it the instruction of the world?

THE OLD CHASING THE YOUNG

We live in a culture that worships youthfulness. Every magazine cover and television show seems to revolve around the beautiful, the young, and the rich. In American society, we have a cream, pill, lotion, or solution for every part of your body that might be aging. We have wigs, liposuction, and plastic surgery available for anyone who can afford it. According to the American Society of Plastic Surgeons, plastic surgeries done in the United States from 2000 to 2016 increased by 132%.[5] Eight billion in revenue was earned from plastic surgery in 2016. Many of these surgeries were for good causes such as helping burn victims, those who've lost limbs, or cancer survivors. But many of these surgeries were performed in an attempt to keep the effects of aging at bay. A *Business Insider* article demonstrates just how much money was spent on plastic surgery in 2016.[5]

Nose reshaping: $1.1 Billion
Breast Augmentation: $1.08 Billion
Facelift: $924 Million
Liposuction: $752 Million
Tummy tuck: $740 Million
Eyelid surgery: $631 Million
Breast lift: $469 Million[6]

We hate getting old in the United States; we see it as a horrible thing. But how does God's Word approach aging? I believe our obsession with youthfulness has led us to trade the wisdom of our elders for the entertainment of the current generation. Because our values are misplaced, our time is spent making an idol out of youthfulness rather than training young hearts to pursue the wisdom of fathers and grandfathers in the home.

The average kid spends several meaningless hours in front of the television each week recording useless stories onto their hard drives. I plead with you to reverse this curse. Read Christian books to your kids. Sing songs with them. Tell them stories from your life and how you came to know God better through certain events. Give them wisdom on how to deal with relationships at school. Teach them that the struggle in math needs to start with prayer instead of just trying harder. Build a Christian culture in your home where Christ is the solution to their problems and where Christ alone is enough. Wisdom comes from you and is to be learned by them. The young are meant to chase the old, not vice versa.

THE WISDOM OF ELDERS "WHEN YOU RISE UP"

The Book of Proverbs is included in what is known as the Poetry and Wisdom books of the Old Testament. The Hebrew word *wisdom* includes the idea of "living skillfully."[7] Knowledge differs from wisdom in that while knowledge is associated with facts, wisdom is living out carefully what you know. Wisdom is the application of knowledge.

Many proverbs are written in the form of a father teaching his son how to live with wisdom. You can almost see a boy sitting at his father's feet as the older, wiser man passes along life lessons. Here are a few examples:

Hear my son, your father's instruction and do not forsake your mother's teaching... (1:8)

My son, if sinners entice you, do not consent... (1:10)

My son, do not walk in the way with them... (1:15)

My son, if you will receive my words and treasure my commandments within you... (2:1)

My son, do not forget my teaching, but let your heart keep my commandments... (3:1)

The book of Proverbs covers a myriad of temptations and instructs the believer on how to avoid the snares of the enemy and engage the culture with integrity. Proverbs 16:31 says, "A gray head is a crown of glory; it is found in the way of righteousness." While our culture tries to hold back the effects of age, the Bible celebrates it, suggesting that age gives insight into what matters most in life.

Actor David Cassidy died November 21, 2017. His last words to his daughter Katie were, "So much wasted time." Cassidy had it all from the world's point of view — fame, money, all the things this world values — but in the end, he realized those earthly treasures were a waste.[8] Teach your kids to love wisdom. Turn off the television, and for a few minutes each day, read and explain a proverb. Be faithful and intentional about viewing life through a biblical worldview. Pass this on to your children so they have the skills to live with wisdom in this fallen world.

Job, another book in the Poetry and Wisdom section, says, "Wisdom is with the aged, and understanding with length of days" (Job 12:12). Are you there yet? Have you gained some wisdom about this world? I remember, early in my marriage, when a guy knocked on the door to our little mobile home. He told me if I let him come in and demonstrate his vacuum cleaner, he would give me a free two liter bottle of Coke. With the smell of the lasagna cooking in the oven, I thought that would be the perfect finishing touch to a fine meal. Well, it was a dumb mistake. The guy's demonstration clearly showed that our vacuum was a piece of junk, and he had the golden nugget. He also offered a discount on that particular vacuum because it was the last one he had to sell that day. Long story short, I ended up buying the vacuum cleaner and wasting a ton of money! Because of my inexperience, I got "taken to the cleaners." I lacked the wisdom to handle the situation. It takes some mistakes and learning from those mistakes to gain the upper hand in situations like that. If a vacuum salesman came to my door today (twenty years later), there would be a totally different outcome.

The Proverbs are the father's preemptive strike against temptations, naivety, and quite frankly, the foolishness that is wired into the human heart. Sons and daughters will have to deal with the temptations the world has to offer. Prepare them so they are not foolish like I was. Our kids will deal with things of eternal significance, not just things like vacuum cleaners.

One way to prepare them is to carefully, slowly, and methodically walk through Proverbs as a family. Schedule a regular time to do this. It may be once a day, or it may be once a week. Everyone's schedule is a bit different, but you won't regret making the effort to have intimate, teachable moments in God's Word with your children. Chapter five will point you to several resources you can use in the home. Also, I have several small devotionals on my website that are free for families to work through together. They can be read aloud with your children, and at the end, they have some discussion questions. Many subjects are covered. I have used them through the years with my family.

Check out www.nextgenerationfaithfulness.com if you need some help to get started.

In my family, we read the Bible or a devotional together every morning before school for about thirty minutes. We also spend some time in family prayer. When they rise up, I want them to start their day with the truth of God's Word. We usually follow a reading program, but at certain seasons we take a break from that and do a book on the Advent, the Reformation, etc. The idea is to give our day and theirs to the Lord "when they rise up."

Remember what Job said: "Wisdom is with aged men…" You can gather this wisdom and then impart it to your children. James 1:5 reminds us that if we ask for wisdom, God will give it to us liberally.

FATHER TIME AND A FATHER'S TIME

I have encountered several fathers during my years of ministry who deeply regretted not spending more time at home with their families. I believe many of them would now trade their successes and vocation accolades to go back and sit at their children's bedsides, speaking truth and listening to their troubles. It is a sad and all too common experience of mine to see an emotional father in his fifties wishing he could change the past while his grown child(ren) are bitter toward him for always choosing his career over them. Hearing this may tug at your heart but bring forth a sense of being trapped. Maybe you have "golden handcuffs" around your wrists. Prayerfully consider this: all the money and success in the world can't replace relationships with your wife and children.

How can you personally and intimately create an atmosphere in the home where Christ is the center if you are never there? I want to encourage you to think and pray about making any needed changes. Providing physically for your family is a critical mission, but being the spiritual head of your family is even more critical.

Have you ever seen a depiction of Father Time? He is pictured as an old man with a long white beard, carrying a scythe for reaping in one hand and an hourglass held horizontally in the other. Father Time is a reminder that when the hour of reaping comes a father's time is over. How will your time have been spent?

MOTHERS

A mother's role within the home is just as critical. The difficulty of work and managing the home can feel overwhelming.

The woman of Proverbs 31 is a tremendous example. She balances the physical needs of the family along with the spiritual. Proverbs 31:15-16 says, "She rises also while it is still night and gives food to her household and portions to her maidens. She considers a field and buys it; from her earnings she plants a vineyard." This woman is engaged in business to help her family. We also read of her in verses 26-27, "She opens her mouth in wisdom, and the teaching of kindness is on her tongue. She looks well to the ways of her household and does not eat the bread of idleness." This woman is focused on spiritual instruction. She knows she must feed her children both physical and spiritual bread.

Mothers, nurturing your children and supporting your husband's plans for the spiritual wellbeing of the family is critical. Consider yourself a steward of your family who will give an account not just for their physical provisions but also for their spiritual ones. How are you doing in this area? When your time comes, if you are one of those fortunate enough to have final words with loved ones in the room, you want to be able to look your children in the eye and know you pursued their spiritual wellbeing before God with all your might.

BALL, NOT BAAL: PERSPECTIVE IN SPORTS

Everyone thinks their kids are going to make it in sports. Well, not everyone, but everyone seems to wish that these days. Before I start this section, I want to say I am not anti-sports. Sports can teach incredible lessons, and I believe young men and women need to be pushed and stretched physically. Sports also help develop mental toughness, teach teamwork and selflessness, and provide many other learning experiences. I played four years of high school football, basketball, and baseball. I went on to play three years of baseball in college until my pitching arm was done. So, I love sports. However, I think we need to bring some perspective to the topic of sports in our culture.

If sports are the center of your home life, then Christ can't be. To determine if sports are taking center stage, you might ask the following questions:

- Does my family routinely skip fellowship with my church in order to participate in sports activities?
- Does my family spend a large part of our free time traveling from game to game, practice to practice?
- Do I think my child needs to play more than one sport? If so, why?

Growing up as a three-sport athlete took an enormous amount of time. Looking back, I probably should have concentrated on one. That definitely would have given me more of a home life with my family and cut down on a ton of stress. I am not sure we would have done more devotionals together or prayed more, but I do know we would have spent more time together.

In the book of 1 Kings, Jezebel led King Ahab and all of Israel astray to worship the gods of Sidon, particularly the false god, Baal. Jezebel's very name in Hebrew contains the name of Baal and meant, "Where is Baal?" People believed an underground struggle took place every winter, and their hope was that Baal emerged the victor. If he did, they believed they would be blessed with a good harvest. If he didn't, they believed they would experience famine. The people cried out in ritualistic worship, "Jezebel!" or "Where is Baal?" until spring eventually emerged.

Some people perform their own "ritual cry" regarding their favorite sports. People are truly obsessed with sports today. Don't be like this! As a parent, you have to bring balance to sports for your children. They don't have the necessary discernment; you must make decisions for their wellbeing. Be prepared to disappoint them sometimes. Parents, I want to encourage you to choose which sports your children play. Letting your kids know from an early age that you will do the picking will help settle the matter early on in their minds. They are not old enough or wise enough to see the implications behind their decisions. Parents picking carefully can help keep God at the center of their home. Don't let "ball" become "Baal" in your family. If you are constantly picking sports over the gathering of God's people, don't be surprised when your children grow up and have no respect for God or his Church. Isn't the God of the universe and his Church more important than the ball team?

"God made me fast, and when I run, I feel his pleasure."[9] You may recognize that quote often attributed to Eric Liddell, the Scottish Olympic runner. He was a great example of an athlete who loved sports but loved God even more. In fact, that quote was written by Colin Welland. He wrote it for Ian Charleson, an actor that played Liddell. "What Liddell did say, and more than once, was that God made him for China."[10] If you have never watched the movie *Chariots of Fire*, please do it! The movie is a good picture of the first part of his life. You can find more about Liddell in Eric Metaxas' book, *7 Men: And the Secret of Their Greatness*.

Because of his conviction that it was wrong to participate in sports on Sunday, Liddell refused to take part in a qualifying heat of the 100-meter dash (his best event) at the 1924 Olympics in Paris. He also gave up running in both the 4x100 and 4x400 meter relays for the same reason. Metaxas says during those events "Liddell was nowhere near the Olympic stadium. He was in the pulpit at the Scots Kirk in Paris, preaching to a large and admiring audience."[11] Liddell received many harsh words from his countrymen because of his stance to put Christ over competing. But Liddell ran for God. He believed his gift came from God and that it would be dishonoring to use it on a day God had said to keep holy. Liddell loved to run, but desired God's glory above the glory of men.[12]

Because his qualifying heat for the 100-meter dash fell on Sunday, he opted to run in the 400-meter dash instead. Liddell gave up the opportunity of competing in his best event, likely giving up a gold medal.[13] Do you know of a professional athlete today who takes the Lord's Day that seriously? Do you know any athlete who would give up a gold medal in order to be present at church on Sunday morning? Even though the 400-meter dash was not Liddell's best event, by God's grace he was able to participate and win gold in his second-best event.[14]

For Liddell, faithfulness to God came before everything else. Liddell ended up doing mission work in China for several years. While there, he was imprisoned during World War II. Metaxas points out that Liddell had the opportunity to leave the prison camp and reunite with his family, but in keeping with his personality, he put priority on others rather than himself. Liddell gave up his freedom, allowing a pregnant woman to be freed rather than himself.[15] He died in prison and never saw his family again. A friend said his last words were, "It's complete surrender."[16] Eric Liddell loved to run, but God made Eric Liddell for China.

Think about the life of David Cassidy and the life of Eric Liddell. Contrast their last words: "So much wasted time" versus "It's complete surrender." When you and your kids decide to engage in sports, read them that story. The Christian life is to be one of complete surrender not wasted time. "If anyone wishes to come after me, he must deny himself, take up his cross and follow me" (Luke 9:27). Sports will most likely be a tiny part of your child's life. The hope we have in Christ is eternal. Develop a longer vision for your child's life than their participation in sports. The priorities you set will pass on to your children. Keep Christ the center of your home.

THE FAMILY TABLE "WHEN YOU SIT IN YOUR HOUSE"

It's not just sports that take a lot of time from families. It could be music lessons, dancing, church activities, or any number of activities. None of these things are inherently bad. I'm simply suggesting it is wise to choose a limited amount of these activities in order to prioritize God and family. You simply can't do everything and at the same time have a home life centered on Christ. Sometimes in order to maintain balance in the home, you must tell your children "no."

I am going to ask a question you may not want to answer. How many times a week do you sit down at a table with your family and eat together? Really think about it.

In the Bible, we see tons of great conversations over meals. We are wired to fellowship with others, and one of the main things we do together is eat. We see this all throughout Scripture. Jesus ate with the multitudes (Matt. 14:13-21), tax collectors and sinners (Mark 2:13-17), and his disciples (Mark 14:12-25). Jesus used the intimacy of eating with sinners to draw them to himself (Luke 5:29-32). Paul also gives us a warning about the intimate practice of eating as well. Christians are forbidden to eat with anyone who claims to be a brother or sister and is living a consistent life of sin (1 Cor. 5:11).

Because of the joy food brings, the family table can be a great place to talk about spiritual things. In the past, I have chosen to read a small proverb or story before my family sat down to eat together, and then we just talked through our day. If you are constantly overbooked and going from one thing to the next, this will be very difficult for you. Eating out for the majority of your meals can make spiritual conversations difficult as well.

Think about mealtimes in your home. Are there ever any calm, unhurried meals where you can all chat about your day and talk about what God is doing in your life? Meals together could be a good time for you to visit, encourage, and speak truth into each other's lives.

5 MINUTES! "WHEN YOU LIE DOWN"

All my kids have wanted alone time with just me or my wife since they were little. There are five of them, so this can be a difficult task. A few years ago, when they were ages eleven all the way down to two, I decided to give one of them five minutes at the end of each day to spend with me alone. At first, I thought the kids would think they were getting hosed on time, but they came to love the idea. I say five minutes, but in reality, it probably averages out to more like fifteen minutes. It's a special time for me to connect with each of my kids, one at a time, to make sure I have their hearts. When things are going well, we may just play a game together. When something is bothering them or me, we talk about it. Sometimes we eat cookies or play a game on my phone. If I'm not totally consistent, the kids always seem to remind me. If we miss a day and the schedule gets messed up, the kids will fuss with each other over this seemingly insignificant amount of time.

Now, you might think they just don't want to go to bed, but some of the best conversations I have ever had with my kids' hearts took place during this time. I have shared this idea with other families, and they have discovered the same thing. Keeping Christ the center of your home may happen during that five minutes when you get to talk with your child about the Savior or about whatever is going on in their lives. Look them in the eyes, ask them how they are doing, and then, LISTEN.

I can't think of a better passage of Scripture to end this chapter than Psalm 78:1-8. It starts with a call for families to be faithful to pass down the tenets of the faith to the next generation, then it tells the story of what happens when the gospel is ignored and not passed down. Here is the initial plea:

Listen, O my people, to my instruction;
Incline your ears to the words of my mouth.
I will open my mouth in a parable;
I will utter dark sayings of old,
Which we have heard and known,

And our fathers have told us.
We will not conceal them from their children,
But tell to the generation to come the praises of the Lord,
And his strength and his wondrous works that he has done.
For he established a testimony in Jacob
And appointed a law in Israel,
Which he commanded our fathers
That they should teach them to their children,
That the generation to come might know, even the
     children yet to be born,
That they may arise and tell them to their children,
That they should put their confidence in God
And not forget the works of God,
But keep his commandments,
And not be like their fathers,
A stubborn and rebellious generation,
A generation that did not prepare its heart
And whose spirit was not faithful to God.

— Psalm 78:1-8

Questions to reflect on from this chapter:

1. Is my home one that reflects my love for God and the gospel? Have I properly understood my role as mother or father to worship God in the home?
2. Have I bought in to the culture's belief that everything "youth" is the best? Have I properly understood that I should be intentionally growing in wisdom and imparting this to my children?
3. Do I take time to speak truth to my family when they rise up, when they walk by the way, and when they lie down? If not, how can I change this?
4. Are sports too important in my home? Is my kid playing ball or Baal?

Important ideas to remember:

1. Deuteronomy 6:4-9 implies that parenting is a 24/7 job.
2. When we are told to bring our children up in the "instruction" of the Lord, the Greek word there is *Paideia*. *Paideia* implies that interpreting the world through a biblical lens is necessary for all of life.
3. Our culture chases youth while the Bible illustrates youth chasing the wisdom of elders.

CHAPTER THREE

LAW & GOSPEL

One must punish in such a way that the rod is accompanied by the apple. It's a bad thing if children and pupils lose their spirit on account of their parents and teachers.[1]

    Martin Luther

For judgment will be merciless to one who has shown no mercy; mercy triumphs over judgment.

    James 2:13

LOGS AND SPECKS

IN 1999, I WAS TWENTY-TWO YEARS OLD, NEWLY MARRIED, AND driving the vehicle of my dreams. My grandmother had died a year before and left some money to the grandkids; I purchased a black, one-year-old, extended cab Dodge pickup. It was an awesome ride for a college student, and I took meticulous care of that thing.

Heading to a class, I pulled out of the driveway and noticed Shane, a five-year-old neighborhood kid, standing on the side of the road, a big smile on his face, his hands hidden behind his back. As I smiled back and began to pull past him, he drew a huge walnut from behind his back, and with what seemed to be the power of an Aroldis Chapman 105 mph fastball, Shane let that puppy fly at the side of my truck! Not only did Shane have an incredible throwing arm, but that little devil could run as fast as a rabbit. I slammed my truck into park and raced after Shane.

Have you ever found yourself doing something you shouldn't, but you were so caught up in the heat of the moment you just didn't think? Like, maybe I shouldn't have chased a five-year-old through the neighborhood toward his house yelling at him the whole way? Maybe I, the adult, should have walked calmly to the front door, knocked gently, and when it opened articulated carefully and thoughtfully the incident and asked his mother or father to rectify the situation? Should-a, would-a, could-a, right?

Shane darted through the back door, slamming it on my arm as I reached through to grab him. Because of Shane's yelling (or mine, I'm not sure which) his mom appeared at the back door and swooped Shane up in her arms. You can imagine her look of distress at what she saw. I explained the situation and watched with delight as she spanked Shane before I even left the room. I felt in the moment that some justice was doled out for the sin against my dear truck. When Shane sinned against me, what did I want for him? I wanted him to pay for what he had done. I wanted him to feel the full force and weight of his sin. I wanted justice!

Thirteen years earlier, I was a nine-year-old with some buddies at a church barbeque at (you guessed it) Paul Benne's house. Paul had a lush, beautiful farm with many acres, timber, and some open fields and ponds. It was a place you could really see God's handi-work in nature. The church family was enjoying the fine weather, hanging out, and getting ready for an old-fashioned cookout. One man in attendance was Richard Bess. I don't remember much about Richard other than he was a really nice man. Always kind and patient, he and his wife, Sue, worked with the church teens. As my buddies and I crested a hill, we noticed Richard a couple hundred feet from us. He lay on the shore of a pond, his hands behind his head, taking in the beautiful sun rays, relaxing and enjoying the day.

His fishing pole gently rested to his side, the bobber floating on the water.

I'm not sure whose idea it was, but someone suggested we throw a rock to see how close we could get it to Richard. Well, I had a good arm, and I decided I would be the guy. I threw that rock. It struck Richard right in his ribcage! I heard a grunt and a yell I will never forget. Guess what else happened? I RAN! I was Shane!

When Richard caught up to us inside the house, he asked who threw the rock. No one took responsibility. Richard was angry and hurt. I can still remember him pulling up his shirt and showing the spot where he was hit. Man, he got nailed! I never paid for that sin. Richard, instead of pursuing it to the end, shamed us, walked off, and never mentioned it again. He truly gave us mercy we didn't deserve.

Jesus tells a parable in Matthew 18 that is very important for us to drink in deeply. It's referred to as the parable of "The Unmerciful Servant." Please read through this parable, and you will quickly see how the previous stories relate.

THE UNMERCIFUL SERVANT

Then Peter came and said to him, "Lord, how often shall my brother sin against me and I forgive him? Up to seven times?" Jesus said to him, "I do not say to you, up to seven times, but up to seventy times seven.

"For this reason the kingdom of heaven may be compared to a king who wished to settle accounts with his slaves. When he had begun to settle them, one who owed him ten thousand talents was brought to him. But since he did not have the means to repay, his lord commanded him to be sold, along with his wife and children and all that he had, and repayment to be made. So the slave fell to the ground and prostrated himself before him, saying, 'Have patience with me and I will repay you everything.' And the lord of that slave felt compassion and released him and forgave him the debt. But that slave went out and found one of his fellow slaves who owed him a hundred denarii; and he seized him and began to choke him, saying, 'Pay back what you owe.' So his fellow slave fell to the ground and began to plead with him, saying, 'Have patience with me and I will repay you.' But he was unwilling and went and threw him in prison until he should pay back what was owed. So when his fellow slaves saw what had happened, they were deeply grieved and came and reported to their lord all that had happened. Then summoning him, his lord said to him, 'You wicked slave, I forgave you all that debt because you pleaded with me. Should you not also have had mercy on your fellow slave, in the same way that I had mercy on you?' And his lord, moved with anger, handed him over to the torturers until he should repay all that was owed him. My heavenly Father will also do the same to you, if each of you does not forgive his brother from your heart.

Matthew 18:21-35

The very thing I wanted for Shane — the law — I did not want for myself thirteen years earlier. I was like the unmerciful servant who wanted to tap into mercy for my foolish childhood mistake but didn't want the same for an even younger child. It's probably true for us all that at times we want the law for others but the gospel for ourselves. Notice the warning at the end of the parable: "My heavenly Father will also do the same to you, if each of you does not forgive his brother from your heart." Forgiveness is not an option. It is an expectation of everyone who has been born again. Jesus in the Sermon on the Mount said, "For if you forgive others for their transgressions, your heavenly Father will also forgive you. But if you do not forgive others, then your Father will not forgive your transgressions." This passage is not teaching that unless you do the "good work" of forgiveness you cannot be saved, but rather that if you are saved you will do the good work of forgiveness. Forgiving others is a natural outflow of being forgiven. Tough stuff isn't it?

Jesus also says in the Sermon on the Mount, "Or how can you say to your brother, 'Let me take the speck out of your eye,' and behold, the log is in your own eye? You hypocrite, first take the log out of your own eye, and then you will see clearly to take the speck out of your brother's eye." Shane hitting my truck was a "speck." My hurting a person (Richard) was a "log." I'm not saying Shane didn't need disciplined. He did, but I needed to remember that while I shouted for the law to be carried out, Christ was whispering, as always, the gospel message.

LAW OR GOSPEL OR BOTH?

Laws are immutable truths from God. There is no changing them. Laws are brute fact — cold, hard, and true. They help the sinner desire a pardon they don't deserve. Laws reveal the truth that actions such as lying, stealing, and murdering are wrong.

We as parents need to be careful to use the law the way it was meant to be used. What do I mean? Paul says, "We know that the Law is good, if one uses it lawfully..." (1 Tim. 1:8a). The law was not given as much for self-improvement as it was given to point out our need for Christ. Galatians 3:24 says, "Therefore the Law has become our tutor to lead us to Christ, so that we may be justified by faith." Don't use the laws of God as the "end all" for your children.

The laws are good, but we are not (Rom. 3:10-12). Keeping God's law perfectly is impossible for us. This is why Jesus came (Matt. 5:17). He did what we could never do by keeping the law of God perfectly. He was the second Adam who chose to fulfill God's holy will. To expect your kids to keep God's laws perfectly will lead to bitter disillusionment and skepticism of his mercy.

Martin Luther, who tried to please God in the flesh, said later when reflecting upon his days in the monastery: "If ever a monk got to heaven by his monkery, it was I!"[2] Luther tried everything. He beat himself, laid in the snow until passing out, and starved himself, but ultimately, he realized it was the kindness, grace, and mercy of God's gospel that he needed. When Luther realized he was forgiven through the gospel by faith alone in what Christ had done, he said it was as if "the doors of paradise swung open and [he] walked through them!"[3] Remember Galatians 2:16: "By the works of the Law, no flesh will be justified." Pray your kids swing open those doors of paradise! But how do we get them there?

CHILDREN CONVICTED BY THE SPIRIT

If the law is a "tutor to lead us to Christ" (Gal. 3:24), then we should use it that way. Sometimes kids need to know how they have offended God and what laws they have broken. In these cases, use the law to tutor them. Other times, they come to this realization through the convicting power of the Holy Spirit.

Children already grieving their sin do not need to be clobbered over the head with God's law. They know it, and they need the gospel. They need to be reminded that the remedy for sin is a person who loved them so much that he died in their place and rose again to have complete fellowship with them. Moving forward, they must exercise faith in his absolute goodness and in their need for him at all times. Parents, when your children realize their sin and are dealing with it, you become preachers of the gospel.

One early Monday morning, I was setting up the chapel at school before the students arrived. I noticed one girl following me around at a distance, acting strangely. I finally asked if she needed anything. She burst into tears, and I was shocked to hear her ask, "Mr. Winslow, can you ever forgive me?" This was a quiet, timid, well-behaved child. I had never heard a teacher say one negative word about her or seen any rebellion in her life. She was a model fifth-grader. I told her to meet me in my office so we could talk. Once there, she told me that Friday afternoon she had reached into her desk and got the answers to cheat on her Latin test. She hadn't been able to sleep all weekend and had to get it off her chest. Right now, while typing this, I am getting teary again. It was God the Holy Spirit at work in this girl. She didn't need the law at this point. She was ready for the gospel. I talked with her about the love Christ had for her and that I, of course, forgave her. I watched that girl grow into a godly young woman, and seven years later I watched her graduate. I thank God that he gave me the chance to be the gospel in that situation.

In another situation a few years ago, my kids were throwing a ball around in the house. After watching this for a few minutes, I realized they weren't that good at controlling the ball and told them to stop. Laura threw the ball one more time, hitting the huge clock on the wall. It fell to the floor, and the glass shattered. She instantly started crying and asking for forgiveness. Not only did it startle her and the rest of us when the glass flew everywhere, but she immediately knew her folly. For me to yell wasn't going to show her anything that the natural consequence of not honoring me in the moment hadn't already shown her. We had a great talk about the sin of the moment and the grace of forgiveness. This same child once decided to call 911 while at a friend's house. By the time I found out, a police officer had already talked with her. When she saw me, the tears were flowing. Instead of being angry, I calmly asked if she learned her lesson. She was broken-hearted over doing something so foolish. The law had already done its work in her heart, and she really desired forgiveness. Who was I to not quickly extend it?

CHILDREN INDIFFERENT TO SIN

However, when sin is not realized or being dealt with, we must handle our children differently. When children are cold to truth and indifferent toward a holy God, make sure to give them the law "in love."

Sometimes, students sent to my office in trouble showed no signs of conviction for sin. I could almost visualize the little boys sitting there in a wife-beater shirt with a half-smoked cigar hanging out of their mouths saying, "Bring it!" To the best of my abilities, I tried to explain to these kids that they had offended and broken fellowship with others. I told them how God viewed these actions, making sure to lay the responsibility on them. If they wanted to be judged by God's absolute goodness (the law) then they would fall grossly short of the standard.

We all will be judged by God's absolute perfect standard just like Jesus if we determine not to choose the grace of the gospel. James 2:10 says, "For whoever keeps the whole Law and yet stumbles in one point, he has become guilty of all." Since none can keep the whole law, we are all guilty. Point out to your children that you have the same need. Call them to repentance, reminding them that pride destroys. We are all rebels who need to be reconciled. Lovingly, faithfully, and patiently encourage your kids to be reconciled to God. Remember, you are Christ's ambassador. Pray God will convict their hearts of their sin and of their need for the mercy of Jesus. When they are ready, walk them through what confession and repentance look like.

Sometimes an indifferent child needs a spanking. Yes, I said it. A spanking. Proverbs 22:15 says, "Foolishness is bound up in the heart of a child; The rod of discipline will remove it far from him." Have you tried really hard to reason with your three or four-year-old about why it's not wise to run in the Walmart parking lot? Did they give you that blank I-don't-understand stare? It could be because they lack enough life experience to understand the undeniable logic of your statement. You could try explaining to them why they should honor your wishes and that disobedience is sinful and then watch them commit the same sin again the next hour. This is when a swat might be helpful. I'm not talking about a beating. I'm talking about a little swat on their bottom where God gave them a little more padding. My good friend from Africa shared this common Zambian saying: "Children's ears are on their butts." Sometimes this is true.

When a child is old enough to reason and understand the law of God, you should naturally move toward conversational correction. I have known people who believe it is okay to spank their seventeen-year-old daughter or son who still lives with them. That's wrong and a little odd. Spanking should be used responsibly with little ones who make foolish choices at a risk to themselves and others. They may need a swat, and you shouldn't be afraid, as a parent, to give them one, no matter what the culture says. However, you should never spank out of anger. If you can't control your temper, this is not a discipline option for you. A spanking is all business; it's not personal. You are trying to communicate an important point that gets the attention of your child not hurts them. If your conscience won't allow you to spank, follow your conscience. If you do spank, remember that once the little one is paying attention, it's time to move directly into the gospel of forgiveness. The spank is never to be the end in itself. It is used to gain the attention of the little one so fellowship may be restored.

WORK AT DISCERNING WHAT DISCIPLINE SHOULD LOOK LIKE

Discernment in discipline is incredibly important. What does a kid need in the moment? Does he need the law or the gospel? For eleven years, I was the headmaster of a classical Christian school in Missouri. I was there the day the school opened with twenty-seven students. Eleven years later, we had grown to over 150. Needless to say, the more students there were, the more sin, trouble, and discipline we had. Sometimes, it was hard to know how to discipline a kid. Other times, it was clear what they needed.

The responses of the students sent to my office varied significantly. Was the student crying because he got caught, or was he genuinely feeling the weight of his sin? Was the student indifferent because he didn't get it or because he didn't care? Trying to discern a student's reaction was difficult.

One fifth-grader in trouble came into my office with a huge smile on his face. You want to get under my skin? Disrespect a teacher and then smile about it! I harshly spoke to him, only to find out later from his dad that when he was under stress or great pressure, even fear, he smiled! Sometimes he even laughed!

We need to be students of our children. We need to read them, learn their weaknesses, and recognize their besetting sins so we know how to approach them with the tutor of the law and lead them to the gospel.

DON'T ASSUME TOO MUCH (A DIFFERENT SHANE)

One Friday evening when we were in second grade, my friend Shane and I decided to walk on top of the high school building. We were running around the track, just goofing off, when we noticed the football bleachers pushed up very close to the building. We figured if we climbed to the top of those bleachers and jumped, we could get onto the roof, which I am guessing was ten to fifteen feet off the ground. It was a stupid idea! However, we were correct; it could be done.

After we walked around the roof for a while, a high school janitor spotted us and yelled at us to come down. He was really mad! I don't think either of us knew why. We never talked about how not to get caught or what would happen if someone saw us. We just went for it! Shane and I climbed down and forgot all about it. Monday at school, Mr. Gibbons, the principal, called me to his office. The janitor, Mr. Gibbons, and our parents all assumed Shane and I were up to no good. But, honestly, we were just foolish boys who needed to understand the gravity of our decision. We had no idea we even needed forgiveness. We had no idea we had transgressed the law by risking our lives and doing something no one was allowed to do. We first needed to feel the weight of our sin so we could understand our need for forgiveness. If the janitor hadn't caught us, I guarantee we would have climbed back onto that roof another day. We didn't know we had done something wrong. We needed to know that we in essence "broke the law." This resulted in our needing to be restored. We needed forgiveness with a directive to live in the truth.

This is the kind of discipline that can be the most frustrating to parents. It's the kind that starts with assuming our kids know more than they do about the world. When they don't and something happens, we are shocked when they do something really dumb. This, however, provides an opportunity to walk through the law and the gospel with them, carefully explaining the transgression and its danger (both physical and spiritual). Tell them how this sin separates them from others and how they need to be forgiven and restored.

Paul talks about a sorrow that leads to death and a sorrow that leads to life. In 2 Corinthians 7:10 he says, "For the sorrow that is according to the will of God produces a repentance without regret, leading to salvation, but the sorrow of the world produces death." We want to see in our children sorrow according to God's will that leads to repentance without regret.

SHOWING "GOSPEL" IS SHOWING FORGIVENESS

One of the hardest parts of the Christian life is to release someone's sin and not bring it up again. This is doubly hard in the home. We are always there together, and because we have a memory, things begin to add up in our mind. Paul, speaking about love in 1 Corinthians 13:5, says, "It does not dishonor others, it is not self-seeking, it is not easily angered, *it keeps no record of wrongs*" (emphasis mine).

Forgiveness is one of the most difficult, if not the most difficult, undertaking in everyday, practical life for the believer.

I remember reading about the murder of Amanda Blackburn in 2015. She was pregnant and only twenty-eight years old. While her fifteen-month-old son, Weston, was upstairs in a crib, she was brutally murdered by three men. I was angry about what had happened to this young woman. Soon afterward, I was shocked at the response her husband Davey posted on Facebook. He said, "Though everything inside of me wants to hate, be angry, and slip into despair, I choose the route of forgiveness, grace, and hope." Did he just say forgiveness, grace, and hope? Incredible. This man's beautiful wife and unborn child had been ripped from him, leaving him alone with his small son, and yet he was able to forgive!

This kind of forgiveness only comes from knowing Christ. This same Christ said, "But I say to you, love your enemies and pray for those who persecute you, so that you may be sons of your Father who is in heaven; for he causes his sun to rise on the evil and the good and sends rain on the righteous and the unrighteous" (Matt. 5:44-45). Jesus tells us to love our enemies. This is what Davey decided to do.

He went on in the same post to say, "If there is one thing I've learned from Amanda in the ten years we were together, it's this: choosing to let my emotions drive my decisions is a recipe for a hopeless and fruitless life. Today I am deciding to love, not hate."[4] Now, compare that sort of redemptive love to how you talk to your children and how they talk to each other. Compare that sort of redemptive love for an enemy to the petty, goofy, upsetting things that get us all riled up in family life. Most things we fuss over we can't even remember the next day. Still, they create friction between us that hinders fellowship, and if they are not resolved, they lead to bitterness.

Sit down with your kids after they finish fussing and gently recount a story like Davey's. Ask them if they would have the ability to do what he did. Stories like Davey's are common in the Christian faith. In times of stress within the family unit, we need to call on these stories from giants of the faith as models for everyday life. People like Davey are modeling their master. It was Jesus who cried out, "Father forgive them, they know not what they do!" This, as he was dying on the cross! Stephen, the first early church martyr, said something similar at his stoning, "Lord, do not hold this sin against them!"

In a similar story years earlier, Elisabeth Elliot's husband, Jim, was murdered by the Waodani tribe in Eastern Ecuador. The very people he loved enough to take the gospel to murdered him and several friends. Instead of hating the Waodani, Elisabeth decided to love. She continued the work of her husband by taking the gospel to this spiritually lost tribe. As a result of her love and patience, many of the tribe converted to Christianity.[5] Jim wrote in his diary, "He is no fool who gives what he cannot keep to gain what he can never lose."[6] Jim was willing to give his life to receive a reward he could never lose. Elisabeth showed the Waodani what this faith Jim preached about looked like in action.

The above stories illustrate that on a horizontal level, some of the worst atrocities can be forgiven by our fellow men and women. If these people forgave murderers, it should be simple for Christians in the home to forgive the brother who never puts in a new toilet paper roll or eats the last of the Cocoa Puffs. In order for our children to learn to forgive, we must first model forgiveness. We can't tell great stories like the ones above and, at the same time, keep bringing up the shortcomings, failures, and past sins we supposedly forgave. If we are doing this, we are not teaching them biblical forgiveness. Elisabeth Elliot along with Davey Blackburn, Saint Stephen, or even Jesus, could have turned bitter against their enemies. Instead, they determined to love them because of the gospel of forgiveness. With real forgiveness, you must let the transgression go.

TEACH YOUR KIDS TO LOVE EACH OTHER'S WEAKNESSES

I have to admit it. My wife locking her keys in the car used to drive me crazy. One particular year, she seemed to either lock them in the car or lose them once a week. Instead of lovingly bearing with the problem, I immediately began telling her how to solve it — where to put them in the house or when she walked into a store, etc. My frustration was evident and so was hers.

We had several young kids, and she had a lot to manage. Going to the grocery store was the equivalent of trying to land the lunar module. In the midst of chaos and car seats, she was losing her keys, and then she had to make that dreaded phone call to me for help. When I realized that phone call to me was dreaded, I saw my sin. I swore before God to take care of her. I was supposed to be her champion. Instead, I was ticked off and bothered by the situation.

Had I forgotten some of the simplest biblical truths about man and woman? God made Eve to be a "helper suitable for him" (Gen. 2:18). The word for helper can mean: "like opposite him."[7] Everything I'm not, she is, and everything she's not, I am. In this situation she needed me to lovingly come beside her. She needed me to be what she was not. This should have been an honor, and I viewed it as a nuisance. I had the opportunity to be like Christ, but because of my selfishness in that season of life, I blew it. God later revealed this to me through his Word and opened my heart to finally listen. Galatians 6:2 says, "Bear one another's burdens, and thereby fulfill the law of Christ." When our frustration at someone's weakness turns to helping them carry their burden, we become more like Jesus. When I began to look at my strengths as helping offset her weakness, I understood that my strengths are not just for me. They were given to me so I could give them away. When my wife likewise uses her strengths unselfishly for my weaknesses, I see

God's grace being given to me. This has helped us to love one another better.

HIS POWER IS PERFECTED IN MY WEAKNESS

Most sins between my children begin as a simple annoyance. Someone says something or does something that isn't a big deal, but then the annoyance grows, and pretty soon someone loses his/her temper over something silly. Sound familiar?

The apostle Paul mentions something in the second letter to the Corinthians that has baffled scholars for years. Without telling us exactly what it is, Paul refers to something that continuously torments him, calling it his "thorn in the flesh" (2 Cor. 12:7). Many have tried to guess what plagued Paul. Some think it may have been a disease or sickness while others speculate it may have been a person. Whatever it was, Paul was desperate to shake it. God, however, wanted him to have the weakness. Paul says:

> Concerning this I implored the Lord three times that it might leave me. And he has said to me, 'My grace is sufficient for you, for power is perfected in weakness.' Most gladly, therefore, I will rather boast about my weaknesses, so that the power of Christ may dwell in me. Therefore I am well content with weaknesses, with insults, with distresses, with persecutions, with difficulties, for Christ's sake; for when I am weak, then I am strong.
>
> 2 Corinthians 12:8-10

God's grace is perfected in our weaknesses. Whatever the thorn, Paul extrapolated from it the truth that in any weakness he might have had, God's grace was enough. More than that, he said when he was weak, God made him strong through grace.

It's always easier to see someone else's shortcomings rather than our own. Like Amy with her keys, I could see clearly the solution to the problem. What I couldn't see was that I was being a jerk. (Though Amy clearly did!) If I had wanted to be like the God I serve, I should have sought to be the strength in her weakness. If I had followed that model, it would have led to great harmony in our home. Ultimately, as Paul said, God is our source of strength in times of great difficulty. We tend to add to others' difficulties in our selfishness and lack of understanding. But God has given us the opportunity to lessen their burdens by loving them through their weaknesses.

If your kids have come to faith in the gospel, encourage them to see themselves as a helper for their siblings' weaknesses. Explain to them that every person has a "thorn" in areas others don't. Teach them to be empathetic toward the weaknesses of others, lovingly correcting sin and gently speaking truth. Guide your children toward becoming a source of strength, and model this by being a source of strength for them. Offer solace when they have trouble repenting and openly invite others to speak into your own life. Dads and moms, if we can't take responsibility for our shortcomings and mistakes, how do we expect our kids to do so? In Matthew 7:2, Jesus said that the same measure you use to judge others will be used to judge you. Everyone in a family has blind spots. Work together to overcome them with grace and humility. Be strength in the weakness of others.

Questions to reflect on from this chapter:

1. Am I giving grace to my children when they realize they have offended the law, or do I beat them up with the truth?
2. Do I give the law to my kids when they are indifferent to sin? Am I carefully explaining to them what it means to have a broken relationship with God (vertically) and with our fellow man (horizontally)?
3. Am I teaching my children to work at being the strength in each other's weaknesses? Am I doing this for others? Have I realized that even I have blind spots and people give me grace?

Things to remember from this chapter:

1. Do not be like the unmerciful servant when your child sins. The golden rule is, "Do unto others as you would have them do unto you." You like to receive the grace of forgiveness; be quick to dispense it to your children.

2. When a child is clearly under conviction from the Holy Spirit (realizing he has offended God's law), preach to him the gospel. Remind him of the forgiveness and freedom found in Jesus! Remember, sometimes a child is not sad because of conviction but sad because he got caught. Discern the difference.

3. When children are indifferent to their sin, they may need the law spoken very clearly to them. If they are really small, they may need a swat to help them understand. If they are older, logically explain to them what it means to sin against a Holy God and their need for reconciliation. Neither you nor I can change a heart. Turn to God in prayer!

4. Don't assume your children are sinning with their eyes wide open all the time. Sometimes, the sheer orneriness of internal sin occurs without kids even knowing it.

5. Model forgiveness for your children. Don't keep bringing up past infractions if they have been dealt with. Be a model of Jesus' love and forgiveness.

6. Because we all have sin and blind spots, we should lovingly point them out to each other and offer strength in others' weaknesses, remembering we have our own issues that require grace.

CHAPTER FOUR

THE DISCIPLINES: BE FAITHFUL!

But Jesus himself would often slip away to the wilderness
and pray.
> Luke 5:16

But his delight is the Law of the Lord and in his Law he meditates
day and night.
> Psalm 1:2

... not forsaking our own assembling together, as is the habit of
some, but encouraging one another; and all the more as you
see the day drawing near.
> Hebrews 10:25

Can we expect the flames of our worship of God to burn brightly
in public on the Lord's Day when they barely flicker for Him in
secret on other days?[1]
> Donald S. Whitney

EVER SINCE MY GIRLS WERE TINY, I'VE TOLD THEM HOW BEAUTIFUL
they are. My daughter Anna, the oldest, has heard it the longest.

When she wakes up in the morning, I say, "Good morning, Beautiful." If she is getting ready for a school Christmas concert or has on a new Easter Sunday dress, I say, "Man, you are gorgeous!"

When she was eight or nine, she started saying, "Dad, you just say that because you're my dad." Sometimes she says, "All dads say that to their daughters." Recently, though, after she turned eleven, she and I were on a trip to her grandmother's house.

She said to me, "Hey Dad, you know how you always tell me how pretty I am and everything?"

"Yeah," I said.

She said, "Well, I was looking in the mirror the other day, and I noticed that you were right. I am pretty."

I tried not to laugh and replied, "I told you so."

I tell you that funny little story because there are some truths we just have to arrive at ourselves. I can tell you how prayer time alone with God is great. I can tell you about discovering treasure while reading the Word alone. I can tell you it's possible for you to lead your families to experience God in real ways, but until you look in the mirror, see it for yourself, and experience that it's true, I'm just another guy telling you something. There is no substitute for experience.

Before I talk about the disciplines, I want to make it clear that the disciplines don't earn us God's favor or make us right with him. Author Dr. Kara Powell explains why the disciplines are critical in her book, *Sticky Faith*: "Spiritual disciplines do not make us righteous because we do them, but rather they put us in a position to be drawn into trusting Christ more fully."[2] The disciplines change us from the inside out.

I believe Christian families today deeply desire to shine brightly for Jesus, to have others look at their lives and easily see something different, something we have and they want. I also believe each of us wants to reflect the glory of Jesus through our individual lives and touch the world with his grace and kindness. The ability for us to do this exists. It's not a fairy tale or something only found in the Bible. If you are a Christian, you have the power of the Holy Spirit residing in you (Acts 2).

You may, however, have a simple issue with prioritizing. The next couple chapters are meant to inspire, exhort, and push you a little into making choices that help your family live differently. Dallas Willard was a professor of the School of Philosophy at the University of Southern California. In his book, *The Spirit of the Disciplines*, he said, "All of us can make our daily lives and vocations be the house of God and the gate of heaven. It can and must happen. And it will happen. The living Christ will make it happen through us as we dwell with him in life appropriately disciplined in the spiritual Kingdom of God."[3] He goes on to say, "The disciplines are part of the good news of new life. We should practice them and then invite others to join us there."[4] To invite you to this place, you must first understand that you and I must be disciplined. Our discipline in our spiritual walk with Jesus will inevitably lead to Spirit-filled parenting. When our inner life with God is a priority, we will parent in a way that makes relationship with God a priority for the whole family.

"DISCIPLINE"

You might recoil at that word, but notice how closely related it is to the word "disciple." You might say these words are cousins. Former president of Wheaton college Raymond Edman said:

> Discipleship means "discipline!" The disciple is that one who has been taught or trained by the Master, who has come with his ignorance, superstition, and sin, to find learning, truth, and forgiveness from the Savior. Without discipline we are not disciples, even though we profess his Name and pass for a follower of the lowly Nazarene. In an undisciplined age when liberty and license have replaced law and loyalty, there is greater need than ever before that we be disciplined to be his disciples.[5]

If we took nine random people and made you the tenth, and examined your lives — what you did with your money, time, and resources — and excluded Sunday mornings and Wednesday nights, would there be enough evidence to identify you as a Christian? Faith transforms the person and should be easy to spot.

As I pointed out in chapter one, we have wrongly made the idea of faith more about propositional knowledge and less about lifestyle change. While faith is believing, it is the kind of belief that drives us toward the crucified life. Is something missing in your spiritual life? Do you want to know Jesus better and live for him, but the busyness of your current situation has led you to think this is as good as it gets? What if the intimacy of certain disciplines could transform your relationship with God and others? I believe they can and will if you give them a chance.

The amount of discipline and love the original disciples had for Jesus even unto death serves as an example for our devotion in the spiritual disciplines I will be talking about. Since Americans today live in a time of relative peace as it relates to our religious freedom, we must take full advantage of knowing him and loving him. Our brothers and sisters around the world don't always share these same freedoms. Christians in places like Sudan, Indonesia, and many other countries can only wish for the same gift of freedom we have.

Remember in chapter one when I said the word for disciple means "student?" A good student must be disciplined. The disciplines I cover in this chapter are prayer, Bible reading, and fellowship. There are several more spiritual disciplines, such as fasting and stewardship; however, for our purposes, I am sticking with the basics. For a deeper study on the disciplines, I highly recommend *Spiritual Disciplines for the Christian Life* by Donald Whitney and *The Spirit of the Disciplines* by Dallas Willard.

PERSONAL/PRIVATE PRAYER: A TIME TO MEET GOD

If I'm totally honest, I have struggled the most with the discipline of prayer. My friends and family will tell you that sitting still for very long is difficult for me. I am usually going one hundred miles per hour, or I'm dead asleep.

I know everyone is wired a little differently, but there is a key concept we can all apply from Luke 5:16 shown to us in Jesus' prayer life. Luke says, "But Jesus himself would often slip away to the wilderness and pray." Jesus had a place where no one could disturb him as he spent time with his father. Do you have such a place where you meet God? It is important that we are alone at some point in a place no one can disturb us so we can handle business with God. In the Sermon on the Mount, Jesus instructs his disciples: "But you, when you pray, go into your closet, and when you have shut your door, pray to your Father who is in secret, and your Father who sees in secret will reward you openly" (Matt. 6:6). During private prayer, there is no one to impress or give you the pious pat on the back. It is a conversation between you and the Creator with nothing to gain except a deeper relationship with him.

Some of my sweetest times and biggest victories have come during personal prayer when no one else is around. If you can't calm down, take a few deep breaths and just be quiet for a few minutes. Ask the Holy Spirit to help you focus and begin talking to the Father. First thing in the morning is the best time for me to participate in this kind of personal prayer. Don't pick up any devices; don't watch any television; don't go to the computer! Instead, spend time alone with God and ask him to rule your day. Most of my mornings begin with walking through the simple acrostic of ACTS in my mind, which helps me focus my prayers.

A = Adoration (adoring and thanking God for who he is)
C = Confession (confessing sin and asking for forgiveness)
T = Thanksgiving (specifically naming things I am thankful for)
S = Supplication (interceding on behalf of friends, family, and loved ones)[6]

When I can't focus well, I do a couple other things from time to time. R. A. Torrey in his book, *How to Pray*, says of George Mueller:

One of the mightiest men of prayer would begin praying by reading and meditating upon God's Word until a prayer began to form itself in his heart. Thus, God himself was the real author of the prayer, and God answered the prayer which he himself had inspired.[7]

So, when I wake up distracted, I just begin reading my Bible first. This helps me put some truth into my mind and grow my prayers from the content of Scripture.

Other times I use the prayer book, *Valley of Vision*, which contains short prayers my wife and I pray over each other nearly every day. They are beautiful, meaningful prayers that many times jumpstart my prayer time with God.

Do not grow weary at trying to take the time to pray alone. It can take a while to form a new habit, but if you persist, you will soon look forward to this very sweet time alone with God, and when you don't have it, you will be sorely disappointed. Be persistent in finding a quiet place alone with the Lord.

THE POWER OF PERSONAL PRAYER

James, the brother of Jesus, says: "The prayer of a righteous man accomplishes much" (James 5:16). James had the nickname "camel knees" because he spent so much time on his knees praying before God.[8] What a great example of what it means to come before the Lord.

In his book, *The Hour that Changes the World*, author Dick Eastman tells the story of Susanna Wesley, the mother of Charles and John Wesley, the founders of the Methodist Church. Eastman says: "At her chosen time for spiritual exercise she would take her apron and pull it over her face. Her children were instructed never to disturb mother when she was praying in her apron."[9] No doubt this faithful practice of disciplined prayer, even in her apron, impacted her boys who went on to impact the world in such a dramatic way for Christ.

History is full of such examples of prayer warriors who interceded on behalf of their children and found their prayers to have an impact on those children.

PRAYERS OF A RIGHTEOUS WOMAN

St. Augustine's mother, Monica, fervently prayed for her son to come to faith. One day, Augustine heard a faint voice in the distance saying, "tolle lege, tolle lege," which means "take up and read." At this, Augustine rose to his feet, took Paul's epistle to the Romans, opened it at random, and saw the following verses, "Let us behave properly as in the day, not in carousing and drunkenness, not in sexual promiscuity and sensuality, not in strife and jealousy. But put on the Lord Jesus Christ, and make no provision for the flesh in regard to its lusts" (Rom. 13:13-14). He was overcome with grief because of his sin and began to weep. At that moment, Augustine gave his life to Jesus.[10]

Amelia Taylor, mother of Hudson Taylor, the great missionary to China prayed for her son's conversion for years. Hudson, at age seventeen, seemed indifferent to the gospel. While his mother was away on a trip, Hudson casually picked up a tract called "Poor Richard." He knew the story would end with a devotional. His plan was to read the tract up to that point, then put it down. At the same moment, his mother, who was seventy miles away, felt the urgent need to pray for her son's soul. She instantly hit her knees and prayed for Hudson to believe the gospel. This was Hudson's most crucial moment. God changed his heart, and he did believe. When Hudson's mother returned, he told her he had something he needed to share with her. She said, "I already know. You gave your life to Jesus Christ."[11] What a faithful mom in tune with the Holy Spirit!

Both Augustine and Hudson would have tremendous impacts in building the kingdom of God. We know about these faithful mothers because their sons told us about them in their writings. These faithful women of prayer had an impact on their children that would affect generations.

PRAYERS OF A RIGHTEOUS MAN

In Don Carson's book, *Memoirs of an Ordinary Pastor*, he stresses how important his father's faithful prayers were to his life and that of his brother. Carson talks about his dad (a little-known pastor) and his commitment to personal prayer:

> Dad's practice in private prayer was to kneel before the big chair that he used and pray loudly enough to vocalize, so as to keep his mind from wandering. Outside the door we could hear him praying, even if we could not hear what he was saying. I can remember countless days when he prayed for forty-five minutes or more; strange to tell, at this juncture I cannot recall days when he didn't. Jim recalls barging in on Dad's study unannounced, finding him on his knees praying, and quietly backing out. But the image has always remained with me, especially during my later, rebellious teen years. While walking away from God, I could not get away from the image of my father on his knees, praying for me. It is one of the things that eventually brought me back.[12]

Don Carson is an incredible biblical scholar for the Church with contributions far too many to name. Both Don and his brother Jim credit this simple practice of their father's personal, private prayer life as having a profound impact on their relationships with Jesus Christ. Fathers, pray for your children. Don't give up!

KEEP ASKING

Jesus tells a parable about the persistence of prayer in the Gospel of Luke that merits mention at this point:

> Now he was telling them a parable to show that at all times they ought to pray and not to lose heart, saying, "In a certain city there was a judge who did not fear God and did not respect man. There was a widow in that city, and she kept coming to him, saying 'Give me legal protection from my opponent.' For a while he was unwilling; but afterward he said to himself, 'Even though I do not fear God nor respect man, yet because this widow bothers me, I will give her legal protection, otherwise by continually coming she will wear me out.'" And the Lord said, "Hear what the

unrighteous judge said; now, will not God bring about justice for his elect who cry to him day and night, and will he delay long over them? I tell you that he will bring about justice for them quickly. However, when the Son of Man comes, will he find faith on the earth?

Luke 18:1-8

The widow in this story wore the judge out! Jesus demonstrates how an earthly judge will capitulate to the will of a helpless widow in order to get her to go away. If an uncaring, earthly judge will give justice to a widow, surely God will give his children what they need when they ask! Persist in your prayers! Know that God wants what is best for his children! Jesus said in the Sermon on the Mount:

Ask, and it will be given to you; seek, and you will find; knock, and it will be opened to you. For everyone who asks receives, and he who seeks finds, and to him who knocks it will be opened. Or what man is there among you who, when his son asks for a loaf, will give him a stone? Or if he asks for a fish, he will not give him a snake, will he?

Matthew 7:7-11

If a man doesn't give a "stone" or a "snake" to his child, but loves him enough to meet his needs, then our Heavenly Father will meet our needs to an even greater extent.

PRAY FOR HIS WILL, NOT YOURS

In 2006, I had the opportunity to travel to the Holy Land. It was a great experience, seeing the places I had read about in Scripture for years. As our tour bus neared the Mount of Olives, I had my Bible sitting on my lap, opened to some famous passages in the Gospels, and realized that mountain had several times been a very sad place for our Lord. Before descending the Mount of Olives, our group stopped at a little chapel on top called Dominus Flevit, Latin for "The Lord has wept." Shaped like a teardrop, this chapel was built as a reminder of when Jesus wept over the city of Jerusalem (Luke 19:41).

As we descended the Mount, we came to the place where Jesus was betrayed, a place of intense prayer and mourning for Jesus. His prayer in the Garden of Gethsemane is one of the most powerful moments in Christian history and a defining moment for Jesus. He poured out his heart to his Father in heaven. His betrayal was at hand, his death near. Gethsemane means "the place for crushing oil." Here, giant stones were lowered onto olives to crush the oil from them, making it the perfect place to fulfill the passion prophecies. Isaiah 53:10 says, "But the Lord was pleased to crush him, putting him to grief." The crushing of Jesus was coming, and he knew it. In fact, in his garden prayer he says, "Father, if you are willing, remove this cup from me; yet not my will, but yours be done" (Luke 22:42). Jesus' prayer in this critical moment shows awesome trust in the will of the Father to do what is right.

When we pray, we have to remember not to treat God like a genie in a bottle. He is not waiting in heaven to give us anything we ask as though we were spoiled children. Sometimes he says, "No." I think we can all say we are glad Jesus wasn't spared from Calvary's cross. Of course, the cross was horrible, but it paid our sin debt and purchased eternal life for us. Because Jesus was so in tune with the Father, he was willing to give up his freedom for God's perfect will to be done. I am glad that sometimes God says, "No."

My wife and I struggled with infertility for several years early in our marriage. We tried several medicines, and she even had surgery. Nothing worked, and we were told we would probably never have children. We prayed and prayed and prayed. We cried out to God for children, but he said, "No."

Over time we began to consider adoption. The more we learned about the great need for children to be adopted, the more we began to pray and consider it. Finally, we decided to adopt. We traveled all the way to Novosibirsk, Siberia, and adopted a little boy we named Noah, which in Hebrew means "comfort" or "rest." Noah became comfort for a barren couple.

Two years later, as my wife and I began our second adoption, she walked into the bedroom and told me she thought she was pregnant. I laughed, but soon learned it was no joke. We had three biological girls over the next four years. It was crazy and completely unexpected, but our story began to make more sense to us.

When Noah gave his life to Jesus, and I had the opportunity to baptize him, I thanked God that he didn't give us the fertility we wanted several years earlier. Adoption wasn't initially on our radar, but God had a big plan for a baby boy in Siberia. We must trust that God knows better than we do.

Because our experience through adoption was so great, we decided number five would be adopted as well. He is a little boy from Ethiopia named Nati. When it seems as if God is not answering, many times he is just saying, "Wait." We should ask, knock, and seek, but ultimately pray for God's will in all our requests. 1 John 5:21 sums up well what happens through prayer: "This is the confidence which we have before him, that, if we ask anything according to his will, he hears us. And if we know that he hears us in whatever we ask, we know that we have the requests which we have asked from him."

WHY SHOULD WE READ OUR BIBLE?

God has given us the Bible as his written revelation so we might know his will. He is not giving us the kind of knowledge that just makes us smarter people, but the kind of knowledge that moves from head to heart to actions, thus changing our lives and those around us.

Do you have a set time each day when you read the Word? If not, I want to encourage you to begin taking a little time each day to read God's Word. Psalm 119:105 says, "Your word is a lamp to my feet and a light to my path." People who read the Bible know where they are heading! God has revealed in his Word timeless revelations so we might know his grand plan for humanity.

Do your children know Scripture is important to you? I am not just talking about sending them to Awana or Sunday school. I mean, do they ever see you reading or listening to the Word of God? It is critical for parents to be in the Word at least a little every single day when possible. Even if you just read one chapter of your New Testament a day, you can easily get through the whole thing in a year while setting a good example for your children.

God speaks through his Word. 2 Timothy 3:16-17 says, "All Scripture is inspired by God and profitable for teaching, for reproof, for correction, for training in righteousness; so that the man of God may be adequate, equipped for every good work." The Greek word for "inspired" literally means "God-breathed."[13] The words in the Bible came from God's mouth! This verse also tells us it is profitable in all areas of our life so we might be equipped for service in the building of God's kingdom. Being able to answer our children's questions in a biblical way about relationships, sin, and critical issues is a must for a parent.

Obviously, we will all need council from others at times, but we should work as diligently as possible to be the kind of parents who know the Word of God. "Be diligent to present yourself approved to God as a workman who does not need to be ashamed, accurately handling the word of truth" (2 Tim. 2:15).

It gives us a Biblical worldview....

Who is God? What is God's will? Is God loving? Is God in control?

Who is man? Where does man come from? What is man's purpose?

Can I know God?

What is sin? Where did sin come from? What are the effects of sin?

Why is there pain and suffering?

What happens when I die?

The answers to all these questions are found in Scripture. When you can answer these questions and others like them from a scriptural foundation, you have a biblical worldview. Having a biblical worldview means you see things the way God does. For example, if someone asks, "Why do bad things happen to good people," a biblical worldview tells us that question is theologically inaccurate. We are all under the curse of the effects of sin. We are sinners by nature and sinners by our own actions. Paul tells us: "There is none righteous, not even one; there is none who understands, there is none who seeks for God; all have turned aside, together they have become useless; there is none who does good, there is not even one" (Rom. 3:10-12). So, from a biblical worldview, a better question would be, "Since God is righteous and man is sinful, why do good things happen to bad people?"

Because of our worldview, we know God is not only righteous, but he is also omnibenevolent. Because he is kind, he seeks reconciliation with sinful man. The more a Christian reads his Bible, the more God's Spirit allows the truth of his Word to soak into the believer. Hebrews 4:12 says, "For the word of God is living and active and sharper than any two-edged sword, and piercing as far as the division of soul and spirit, of both joints and marrow, and able to judge the thoughts and intentions of the heart." Scripture is not an antiquated, outdated piece of literature. It is alive and active. It contains the power of the gospel. It speaks life and truth and judgement to the world. It is our source of ultimate truth.

Jesus says in his prayer to the Father in John 17:17, "Sanctify them in the truth; your word is truth." If you and I want to know truth, we must read, study, and learn God's Word. The Psalmist says:

> How blessed is the man who does not walk in the counsel of the wicked, nor stand in the path of sinners, nor sit in the seat of scoffers! But his delight is in the law of the Lord, and in his law he meditates day and night. He will be like a tree firmly planted by streams of water, which yields its fruit in its season and its leaf does not wither; and in whatever he does, he prospers.
> Psalm 1:1-3

The Hebrew word here for "meditates" is also used to describe a bird that coos the same sound over and over again. A biblical worldview is to "coo" out of the Christian, just like a bird singing the same song over and over again. When we are able to answer life's difficult questions because we have immersed ourselves in God's Word, we will truly say with the Psalmist, "How sweet are your words to my taste! Yes, sweeter than honey to my mouth!" (Ps. 119:103).

It honors those who have sacrificed for us....

"Lord! Open the King of England's eyes." Those last words of a man barely into his forties were spoken just before he was strangled to death and burned at the stake.[14] What had he done that was so terrible?

William Tyndale was born just two years after Columbus sailed to the New World during a time of religious tumult. The Protestant Reformation began when he was just twenty-three years old. Tyndale, born with a natural gift in languages and a former student from Oxford University, could easily translate the scriptures from Hebrew and Greek into English. However, there was a problem; at that time, it was illegal to translate the Bible into English. Anyone caught doing so would be executed.[15]

King Henry VIII was a brutal and impulsive king. Angry that the Pope would not annul his marriage and give him a theological pass, Henry broke away from Catholicism and officially started the English Anglican Church.[16] At first, many Europeans were excited about his decision as this was the height of the Reformation period.[17] Some must have wondered if he had changed his former theological positions. In 1521, before his break from the Catholic Church, Pope Leo X had called Henry VIII "Defender of the Faith" because he had written a rebuttal to Martin Luther on the seven sacraments of the Church.[18] Had Henry changed? People quickly realized Henry was less interested in Catholic theology and more interested in getting his divorce sanctioned. Pope Clement VII had rejected Henry's divorce plea.[19]

During this same time, Tyndale developed a growing passion to translate the scriptures into English for the common man. He believed this was his calling. Before his death, he translated the entire New Testament and over half of the Old Testament into English. Eventually, he was betrayed and turned over to the Imperial authorities. Soon after, he was killed. His only crime was translating Scripture into English for his countrymen.[20]

English historian John Foxe in his famous work, *Fox's Book of Martyrs*, includes a great section on Tyndale. Before Tyndale's complete Bible, only portions of the Bible had been translated into English. His translation was so good that it made up a great portion of many other English translations which came afterward. I have often wondered what men like Tyndale would think of Christians today who have little to no desire to read the Bible. He might cry out, "Lord! Open the eyes of the American Christian!"[21]

FAITHFULNESS BEGETS FAITHFULNESS

I believe every Christian mother and father would say they want to pass down a love for the Word of God to their children. The problem is that often parents haven't cultivated that love in their own hearts. I have to admit, the first time I read the whole book of Isaiah I didn't know what in the world he was talking about. Because God is kind, I was able to gather some nuggets of truth from it, but I also knew to really understand his Word, I was going to have to do some work.

I would recommend supplements to accompany Bible reading for parents who need help understanding Scripture. I remember the first time I read Gary Smith's book, *The Prophets as Preachers*. I finally understood what the Old Testament prophets were talking about. It brought them to life for me. That extra work elevated my Bible reading to an entirely different level. I also highly recommend watching the short videos created by The Bible Project, which you can find on their website or the ReadScripture app for mobile devices. Many good Bible commentaries are readily available as well. Another good resource is the *Life Application Study Bible*.

If you find yourself frustrated for lack of understanding, it may take a little work, but with the power of God's Holy Spirit, I can guarantee you will love the scriptures! If you want to pass on faith-

fulness in reading the Word, then you must read the Word yourself.
You and I must practice what we preach. See Proverbs 4:10-13:

> Hear, my son, and accept my sayings and the years of your life will
> be many. I have directed you in the way of wisdom; I have led you
> in upright paths. When you walk, your steps will not be impeded;
> And if you run, you will not stumble. Take hold of instruction; do
> not let go. Guard her, for she is your life.

Passion is contagious. As you are faithful in your Bible reading,
allow the stories to grow your view of God and the world and
become contagious to those around you. Your faithfulness in the
Word will not only impact your family but also all those you
encounter.

FELLOWSHIP

"I love God, and I am a Christian. I just don't like church." You
have probably heard that a time or two if you have been faithful to
invite people to hear the gospel preached where you attend church.
For years, I have met people who say they love Jesus yet want
nothing to do with his bride.

Barna Group is an organization committed to identifying the
spiritual influencers in our culture. According to Barna Group, in
April of 2016, 73% of Americans still identify as Christians, yet only
a fraction of them attend church.[22] The statistics go on to show:

> When a self-identified Christian attends a religious service at least
> once a month and says their faith is very important in their life,
> Barna considers that person a 'practicing Christian.' After
> applying this triangulation of affiliation, self-identification and
> practice, the numbers drop to around one in three U.S. adults
> (31%) who fall under this classification. Barna researchers argue
> this represents a more accurate picture of Christian faith in
> America, one that reflects the reality of a secularizing nation.[23]

Keep in mind that according to this poll, attending church once a month is considered active — a low standard indeed. God has called us to much more than attending church once a month. He has called us to all-out surrender. Jesus said, "If anyone wishes to come after me, he must deny himself, and take up his cross daily and follow me. For whoever wishes to save his life will lose it, but whoever loses his life for my sake, he is the one who will save it" (Luke 9:23-24). Following Jesus is a commitment to deny self. The person who says he doesn't want to go to church is a person who is putting his own personal desire above following Jesus. The scriptures make it clear that God's people were customarily gathering together in the early church on the Lord's Day (Acts 2:42, 20:7; 1 Cor. 16:1-2). Hebrews 10:25 says, "… not forsaking our own assembling together, as is the habit of some, but encouraging one another; and all the more as you see the day drawing near." This passage teaches that our assembling together as a corporate body is important to the Lord.

When Saul met God on the road to Damascus, do you remember what Jesus said? "Saul, Saul, why are you persecuting me?" (Acts 9:4). Jesus had risen from the dead and was seated at the right hand of God, yet he said Saul was persecuting him. What did he mean? To persecute the Church is to persecute Jesus! The Church is his body. Romans 12:5 says, "So we, who are many, are one body in Christ, and individually members one of another." Notice Paul says we are members one of another. Someone who says he is a Christian yet determines not to be joined to the rest of the body is either being disobedient and walking in the flesh or not actually born again.

If you are a parent and you have disconnected yourself from Christ's body, you need to repent and quick march back to the truth. The Church being the body of Christ is used in many other passages. Paul says in Ephesians 3:6, "To be specific, that the Gentiles are fellow heirs and fellow members of the body, and fellow partakers of the promise in Christ Jesus through the gospel…" In Colossians 1:24, Paul says, "Now I rejoice in my sufferings for your sake, and in my flesh I do my share on behalf of his body, which is the Church…"

If I were to cut off my hand, is it still a part of my body? No! People who have willfully removed themselves from fellowship have removed themselves from Christ's body. I have often wondered why a person who claims to be a Christian but has no desire to be with other Christians thinks for one second he would like heaven. What is heaven except the redeemed of Christ spending eternity together? If someone can't spend a few hours with other believers on Sunday morning, there is no way he would want to enter eternity with them.

If you are in the habit of not faithfully attending fellowship with other believers and you have children at home, you don't have to tell your children whether or not fellowshipping with God's people is important. They will see it through your life.

I Love You, I Just Don't Like Your Bride

If calling the Church his "body" isn't strong enough language, the Bible also makes the analogy of the Church being the "bride of Christ" (Eph. 5:22-33). Men, what If I told you that I liked you fine, I just couldn't stand your wife? Do you think our friendship would go very far? Absolutely not. How is it then that someone can say they want a relationship with Christ, but they don't like the Church?

The Church is full of messed up, sinful people. You may have had some bad experiences, but that is no excuse to not serve the body. This messed up Church includes you if you have embraced the gospel. Jesus poured out his blood for the Church. Who are we to say we don't want to be a part of it? Revelation 21:1-2 says:

> Then I saw a new heaven and a new earth; for the first heaven and the first earth passed away, and there is no longer any sea. And I saw the holy city, new Jerusalem, coming down out of heaven from God, made ready as a bride adorned for her husband.

The bride of Christ has been made holy because of the sacrifice of Jesus. For someone to complain about the Church and say he won't attend because of all the hypocrites is hypocritical. Forsaking the assembling together of God's people is a terrible practice if you are called by his name. Love the bride of Christ! When someone does you wrong, forgive as Jesus forgave you. Give grace because you have been given grace. When you think your church has issues (too many committees, not enough programs, not friendly enough — whatever), be the one to stick around and lovingly encourage change.

The early church had plenty of problems, but that didn't keep believers from meeting together and working hard to get through the issues. Acts 2:42 says, "They were continually devoting themselves to the apostles' teaching and to fellowship, to the breaking of bread and to prayer." You and I live in a country where we are free to worship each week. We should be as devoted to fellowship as the early Church. "… To him be the glory in the Church and in Christ Jesus to all generations forever and ever. Amen" (Eph. 3:21).

SPIRITUAL GIFTS

As important as it is to go to church, always remember that you *are* the Church. Church really isn't a place we go; it's a people we are. Many times, as I pointed out in the last section, people stop fellowshipping at their church because of conflict. They stop attending, and in so doing, they take away the specific spiritual gifting the Lord has given them for use in the body. When you decide not to be plugged into a local church, you are taking your God-given gift away from the rest of Christ's bride.

God gives Christians different gifts to balance out the body. Many churches today don't acknowledge the different functions of each of their members. Instead, we think everyone should be like us. Isn't that natural? After all, I'm perfect, right? If someone does something a little differently or is not interested in exactly the same thing we are, then something is wrong with them, right?

In college after studying Greek for a long time, I decided to teach my wife Greek. There was only one problem. She didn't want to learn Greek. She didn't care about Greek. She didn't even care

that Greek existed. I thought there was something wrong with her. I
was into it, so shouldn't she have been? Not necessarily, as I've come
to learn.

God has given us different gifts. It's kind of like when God
created the woman. As I mentioned in the last chapter, when God
created woman, he made a helper "opposite [Adam]." The objec-
tive between a husband and wife is to balance each other and work
together. The shortcomings of the wife should be balanced out in
the husband, and the shortcomings of the husband should be
balanced out in the wife.

My wife has several spiritual gifts, including the gift of serving. I
have to really work on thinking of others first, but for Amy, it comes
naturally. Greek and similar studies come naturally for me. Can you
see how both are needed? We shouldn't look down on each other
but rather understand each other better. We are different for reasons
prepared by God. Like Paul said, we are to mutually encourage
each other with our spiritual gifts. We all have a spiritual gift, but we
need to know when to use it, helping our fellows and making up the
difference where they are not gifted. We also need to understand
when to be quiet and let others do their thing. Romans 12, 1
Corinthians 12, and Ephesians 4 all give lists of spiritual gifts. I
would encourage you not only to attend church but also to use your
gifts to bring glory to God in his Church.

Be disciplined in prayer, in reading the Word, and in fellowshipping with other believers.

Questions to reflect on from this chapter:

1. Have I realized that the call to be a disciple of Jesus
   requires discipline?
2. Am I setting aside personal alone time with God for
   prayer?
3. Am I praying for God's will to be done and not my own?
4. Am I spending purposeful time in the Word of God
   each day?
5. Am I consistent in my church attendance?

6. Am I faithful to love Christ's bride (the Church)?
7. Am I using my spiritual gifts to grow the body of Christ into maturity?

Things to remember from this chapter:

1. Prayer is not just asking God for things. Remember the acrostic ACTS (Adoration, Confession, Thanksgiving, and Supplication) in your prayer life.
2. If you are struggling to come up with prayers, a good prayer book like *Valley of Vision* may be helpful. It is also good to pray the Psalms out loud when struggling to focus.
3. God hears the prayers of his people and answers!
4. The Bible equips us, teaches us to have God's view of the world, honors those who have sacrificed their lives so we might read it, and passes down a godly practice to our children.
5. Christians are part of the body of Christ. Fellowshipping with other believers is not optional.
6. If we love Christ, we love his bride.
7. I have spiritual gifts I can use in the body of Christ. I should be using those for God's glory.

CHAPTER FIVE

FAMILY WORSHIP: WHAT IS IT? HOW DO I DO IT?

If it is disagreeable in your sight to serve the LORD, choose for yourselves today whom you will serve: whether the gods which your fathers served which were beyond the River, or the gods of the Amorites in whose land you are living; but as for me and my house, we will serve the LORD.

Joshua 24: 15

"If we want to bring up a godly family, who shall be a seed to serve God when our heads are under the clods of the valley, let us seek to train them up in the fear of God by meeting together as a family for worship."[1]

C.H. Spurgeon

WHAT ARE YOUR PRIORITIES?

Every family has priorities, things they do that are so important to them that everything else takes a back seat. Consistent patterns in our lives establish those priorities. It could be that going to Cardinals games is a priority to you. When the Cardinals are in town, everything else stops so you can go to their game. Maybe your kid's ballgame schedule takes precedence over everything else, even church life. Maybe sitting down at the family table to share a meal is a priority in the evening, to talk and fellowship about the day with those closest to you. Whatever your priorities, everything else falls by the wayside so you can do what is most meaningful to you.

You may not have thought about your schedule carefully in a while. You may not even realize exactly where your time and money are going, but you and I should constantly evaluate these important pieces of life. *The Westminster Shorter Catechism* starts with the question, "What is the chief end of man?" The answer is, "Man's chief end is to glorify God and to enjoy him forever."[2] Do you glorify God and enjoy him in your home? Is your home ever a place of Bible reading, prayer, confession, and singing to the Lord? If not, why not?

Remember, we don't go to church, we are the Church. We are a people who have been changed from the inside out, a people who "are a chosen race, a royal priesthood, a holy nation, a people for God's own possession, so that you may proclaim the excellencies of him who has called you out of darkness into his marvelous light." (1 Pet. 2:9). Our chief end is to bring him glory. We can do this wherever we are. Reflect on this question: Is worshiping God with your family a priority in your home life? In the following chapter, I will explain what I mean and how you can answer positively.

WHAT IS FAMILY WORSHIP?

Family worship is just what it sounds like: taking time out of your day to worship the living God with your family. You may think you don't have enough time in your day to do this, and maybe you don't. However, if it's important enough to you, you will make it a goal.

Both fathers and mothers need to demonstrate that worshiping God is more important than their own personal agenda. Private devotions with your family should have a place in your life. Men, you are the leaders in your homes. You are not just physical providers; you are to be spiritual providers. "Man lives not by bread alone, but by every Word that proceeds from the mouth of God" (Matt. 4:4). Wives, you are the other half of the parenting team.

Along with your husbands, be thoughtful about sharing with your children from your quiet times, prayer life, and the myriad of experiences that have helped grow you closer to Jesus. Parents, it is a wonderful practice to have your children attend Sunday school and listen to the sermon every Sunday morning! Do your children have a good relationship with their youth minister and the youth group? Great! But if they are not hearing and participating in spiritual things with both parents, you are not doing your job as a husband/wife team. Examples of this include Bible reading, talking through how a Christian should handle situations, and answering spiritually based questions for your children.

Parents, do you know the answers to these questions about your children:

- How often do they read God's Word?
- How is their private prayer life going?
- Are they good with God or having struggles or questions?

A time set aside for family worship can expose what is going on in your children's hearts. Are they happy to be listening to God's Word, or are they checked out? Do they bring prayer concerns before the family, or are they disconnected? Do they join you in singing praise songs to Jesus? Family worship is an awesome time to read, sing, and pray with your family.

I have experienced some of the most powerful times of worship with my family. At times, God has melted our hearts for the sin in our lives, providing a special time of confession, forgiveness, and acceptance. At times, we have washed each other's feet. Sometimes, we just take a few minutes to express what we like about each other. Siblings often get on each other's nerves and say things they regret later. Family worship gives each child a chance to intentionally be kind to their siblings; it gives us the opportunity to pour truth and love into each other's lives. It is a special, sacred time where everything else stops and we love God and each other.

It doesn't have to be long. Our family worship usually lasts fifteen to thirty minutes. It doesn't have to be the same thing every time, either, as you will see in some ideas below. A specific family worship time does not have to be an everyday thing. It should be commonplace, but never a pharisaical ritual.

What we do in our homes is just as important as what we do on Sunday mornings. All of life is worship, not just the few hours you attend church with your family. Because this is true, families should recognize God not just as the God of Sunday, but as the God of Monday through Saturday as well. Family worship is a great time to enter the presence of God with your family. At the beginning of his work, *Confessions*, St. Augustine says, "You have made us for yourself and our hearts remain restless until they find rest in you."[3] We were made for worshiping God. We can keep ourselves busy with things of the world, but ultimately our rest, peace, and hope are found in Christ. Colossians 1:16 says, "For by him all things were created, both in the heavens and on earth, visible and invisible, whether thrones or dominions or rulers or authorities — all things have been created through him and for him." Notice we weren't just created by him, but *for* him. Family worship shouldn't be laborious, obligatory, or something to check off your to-do list. It should be entered into humbly, willingly, and joyfully. Think of it this way: family worship is made for man, not man for family worship. You are free to enjoy it, and I would say to enjoy it as often as you can!

SOMEBODY SAID IT COULDN'T BE DONE

I learned this stanza of Edgar Albert Guest's poem, "It Couldn't Be Done," in junior high while in Mr. Bessleman's art class, and now I can easily quote it by memory:

> Somebody said that it couldn't be done
> But he with a chuckle replied
> That "maybe it couldn't," but he would be one
> Who wouldn't say so till he'd tried.
> So he buckled right in with the trace of a grin
> On his face. If he worried, he hid it.

He started to sing as he tackled the thing
That couldn't be done, and he did it![4]

I was terrible at art. Mr. Bessleman knew all kids weren't gifted artistically, but because of school requirements, every student had to take art! He heard a lot of kids say, "I can't." Any student who uttered those words in that class had to go to the back of the room and read aloud the above poem.

Why do you think I can still quote it from memory? Because I said, "I can't," and I said it a lot in eighth grade art. You may be thinking right now you aren't qualified to lead worship in the home with your family. Don't say, "I can't!" Nothing could be further from the truth. Dads and Moms, you need no special training in order to worship with your family. You don't have to be a theologian or a worship minister.

I will tell you more about what we do in our home to give you some tracks to run on, but make it your own special time once you get comfortable. Here is a sample week of my family's worship time, taken from when I read through 1 and 2 Samuel with my kids.

Monday:
Song: I will trust in you by Lauren Daigle (3 minutes)
Song: Jesus Loves me (2 minutes)
Read: I Samuel 1 (8 minutes)
Prayer: Prayer requests/Prayer (3 minutes)
Total: 16 minutes

Tuesday:
Read: 1 Samuel 2 (8 minutes)
Discussion: Talk through 1 Samuel 2 (4 minutes)
Prayer: Prayer requests/Prayer (5 minutes)
Total: 17 minutes

Wednesday:
Song: In Christ Alone (4 min)
Read: 1 Samuel 3 (5 min)

Discussion: Everyone said something they love about each other (10 min)
Prayer: Prayer requests/Prayer (5 min)
Total: 24 minutes

Thursday:
Too much life happened, and we missed this day.

Friday:
Read: 1 Samuel 4 (8 min)
Family confession: Sin dealt with/Clear the air time (10 min)
Prayer: I said an overarching prayer to close us as we were running a bit behind (2 min)
Total: 20 minutes

Family worship total for the week: 1 hr. 17 min.

We do family worship in the morning before school. We start at 7:20 a.m. after everyone has eaten breakfast, taken showers, and gotten ready for the day. This is our family's way of giving our day to God. It is the last thing we do before we head out the door.

Notice that we missed Thursday morning. Church ran late Wednesday night, and the kids were super tired Thursday morning. Armageddon didn't happen because we missed a day, and the kids were happy for a little extra sleep. I do not recommend the drill sergeant approach. If you make family worship legalistic and miserable for everyone, the long-term effect on your children could be the opposite of what you intend. Hopefully, it is done with the spirit of worship and love.

Sometimes the kids have bad attitudes (this is normal, they're kids). Don't let that distract you from leading your family into the presence of God and his Word. Typically, the kids can't wait to hear what is going to happen next in the story, but everyone has off days. Also, we often take a few minutes at night to read or pray together. This is less planned and more spontaneous.

WORSHIP THROUGH SONG

Make sure your house is filled with Christian music. As an educator in a classical Christian school for eleven years, I learned the power of young people singing.

First, it is an incredible way to memorize things. Kids learn geography, history, Bible, and grammar facts routinely through song. I remember my surprise the first time I heard a group of fifth graders recite forty-eight prepositions, which took them only a week of practicing to memorize. It might take adults longer, but memorizing is still an incredibly useful tool. I have heard people say they can't memorize things only to see them turn on the radio and sing the words to every song. My mom used to say, "Garbage in, garbage out. Good things in, good things out." Remember this as you regulate what your kids listen to in the home. Kids memorize incredibly well. As I pointed out, they are little hard drives, recording everything going on around them. Singing Christian music is a good way for your kids to bring glory to God and put "good things in."

I would encourage you to have a mix of modern music along with some hymns. Books such as the *Truth and Grace Memory Book* come not only with a catechism but also verses to memorize and some classic songs. I have catechized and sung songs from it for years with my family. My copy is held together with duct tape as I am now using it with my fifth child. Cell phones can connect to a louder speaker, and they allow you to choose just about any song during family worship time. With this technology at our fingertips, we can't make the excuse that we don't sing with our family because we aren't "musical." I am a terrible singer, but I love to sing to Jesus. Fortunately for me, my family drowns me out most of the time. Please don't miss this important way of learning truth and praising God. Psalm 100:1-3 says:

> Shout joyfully to the Lord, all the earth. Serve the Lord with gladness; come before him with joyful singing. Know that the Lord himself is God; it is he who has made us, and not we ourselves; we are his people and the sheep of his pasture.

WORSHIP THROUGH PRAYER: THE MANNA BOX

Praying together as a family is a way to submit to God's rule over your home. It should be natural for us to take time during our day and, together with our children, approach Christ's throne of grace.

One practice we have in our home is recognizing and thanking God for answered prayer. During the Exodus, God supernaturally provided manna from heaven to sustain the Israelites (Ex. 16). As a memorial for God's provision during the forty years of wandering in the wilderness, a golden jar containing manna was stored in the Ark of the Covenant (Heb. 9:4). With this in mind, I gave a task to my three oldest children, and they loved it. I had them take an old Nike shoebox and decorate it, put some holes in the sides of it, and write "Manna Box" on the top. Every time God answers one of our prayers, we write it on a piece of paper, date it, and put it in the manna box.

This has revolutionized prayer in our home. The kids are so excited to see God answer their prayers! At the end of the year we have a big party. We open the manna box up and read each of the answered prayers from that year out loud and praise God for what he has done. We eat, we sing, we watch a movie or play games, but that night is a recognition of God's kindness that year. We retire that year's manna box and before the night is over design a new one for the new year.

By recounting answered prayers, you demonstrate to your kids the power of Almighty God in the answering of prayer. I highly recommend this if you want to get your kids excited about praying to God. Parents, pray with your family! Rick Warren once said, "A dad stands tallest when he kneels to pray with his children."[5]

Praying together with our children has been a very sweet time of fellowship with them and with God. Someone who had visited Charles Spurgeon's home once said, "His public prayers were an inspiration and benediction, but his prayers with the family were to me more wonderful still... Mr. Spurgeon, when bowed before God in family prayer, appeared a grander man even than when holding thousands spellbound by his oratory."[6]

WORSHIP THROUGH FAMILY CONFESSION

Every week or two my whole family sits in the living room and spends some time confessing our sins one to another. It is a very calm time when we start with prayer led by me, and then I usually say a few words. We all take a deep breath, and I remind the kids of the famous passage from 1 Peter 5:5:

> You younger men, likewise, be subject to your elders; and all of you, clothe yourselves with humility toward one another, for God is opposed to the proud, but gives grace to the humble. Therefore humble yourselves under the mighty hand of God, that he may exalt you at the proper time, casting all your anxiety on him, because he cares for you.

As the leader, I start the confession time, and here is how it might go:

Dad: Noah, will you please forgive me? I was impatient with you the other day when you forgot to take out the trash.
Noah: Dad, I forgive you. Is there anything I can do to help you?
Dad: Nope, this one was totally on me. I just didn't practice patience. I am going to try to do better. Will you pray for me right now to do better at that?

Noah will then intercede for me. You may notice this is not only a time for confession but also a time to practice forgiveness. It is a time for the family to get things off their chests while keeping in mind the best interests of the other person. Once Noah forgave me, both of us regained the intimacy of relationship we had before the problem. The air is clear, and the relationship is restored. Everyone in the room takes some time to reflect and ask for forgiveness for their sins against each other. This is never forced. If someone doesn't confess or forgive, it is a good gauge for how you might need to speak privately to your child.

Jesus said, "Forgive us our trespasses as we forgive those who have trespassed against us" (Luke 11:4). This is no time for pride. This is a safe place to let down our guard and know there is restorative love in the room. The intention of family confession time is for horizontal reconciliation. 1 John 4:20-21 says:

> If someone says, "I love God," and hates his brother, he is a liar; for the one who does not love his brother whom he has seen, cannot love God whom he has not seen. And this commandment we have from him, that the one who loves God should love his brother also.

In this context, the "brother" refers to a fellow Christian, but isn't it interesting that he would call another Christian brother? Why the analogy? Because the bond between siblings is supposed to be impossible to break. This is why the story of Cain and Abel is so scandalous. The family bond is supposed to be incredibly deep. If you can't love at home, can you love at all? Thus, the Church is called "the bride" of Christ. This is a relationship not made to be broken. Family confession is a time to make sure sibling relationships and maternal and paternal relationships are where they need to be. It is a healthy practice that helps a family come before God and each other with humble hearts.

I believe this part of worship in our family has proved to have the biggest impact on all of us. It has allowed confession, humility, and forgiveness to be front and center in our family. I highly encourage you to practice this in your home.

WORSHIP THROUGH FAMILY MEETINGS/BLESSINGS (30 MINUTES ONCE A MONTH)

About once a month, we have a family meeting in our home. It is a time for us all to bring to each other the positives and negatives we have stored up in our hearts during the month. If someone is annoyed by the actions of another or has noticed inconsiderate behavior we talk about it. If someone did something to help out or brighten someone else's day, we share that. The meeting is about priorities. How are we doing with each of the things we have been given stewardship over? Here is a list we might go through together:

1. Have I been keeping my room clean?
2. Have I been delightful when asked to do a chore?
3. Am I quick to take responsibility for sin?
4. Am I looking to the needs of others and not just myself?
5. Are we as a family bringing glory to God?
6. Is there anything I need to confess or make right with the group?
7. This month I was thankful for this blessing

   _____.

8. This month I was blessed by this person_____. They did

   _____.

This is a time for parents to talk about media concerns, relationship concerns, attitudes, etc. It is also a time to bring up the victories we have seen during the past month and the things our kids did well. We complement and encourage them. Family meetings are a time to both tune up and lift up. I would recommend scheduling these family meetings every month. At the end of the meeting, we gather in the middle of the room, lay our hands on one another one at a time, and ask for God's blessing on the person and their future.

IDEAS ON WHAT TO READ DURING FAMILY WORSHIP:

With little-littles (2-3 years old)

With two and three-year-olds, I would recommend reading a good children's picture Bible. Amy and I used several of these until we discovered one we and the kids really liked: *The Big Picture Story Bible* by David R. Helm. It is very good at showing the master plan of God. My kids loved reading this with us. The illustrations are great, and the text hits the themed highlights of the story God has woven us all into. Just read them a story each day or so, and make it one of the books you consistently read. Be disciplined. Sing with them "Jesus Loves Me" and other similar songs. Begin speaking to your kids about who God is in a big picture way, and remember their hard drive is always spinning. You are being recorded.

The littles (4-6 years old)

Catechism is a great way to start teaching theology to children aged four to six. The word *catechism* comes from the Greek word *katekeo* and means "I instruct." It has been used for centuries in both the Roman Catholic and protestant traditions. Catechism is simply a series of questions and answers on theological truths that parents can ask their child, encouraging them to memorize the answer. Over time, kids can quickly memorize lots of information. I used *Truth and Grace Memory Book* to catechize all my children. This book is a fantastic resource which includes suggestions on Bible memory verses for specific ages, songs, a great catechism in the back, and a place to record the date of completion next to each question and answer your child has memorized. Here is an example of what you can expect:

Q: Who made you? [parent]

A: God made me. [child]

Q: What else did God make? [parent]

A: God made all things. [child]

Q: Why did God make you and all things? [parent]

A: For His own glory. [child][7]

A four or five-year-old can easily memorize a couple of these questions each week in just ten to fifteen minutes of practice each day. I have used this successfully with all five of my children. My now six-year-old son, Nati, is on question 42. We recently had quite the laugh during catechism. Question and answer number eighteen was pretty tough for him. Here was my question and his answer:

Q: Of what did God make Adam and Eve?

A: God made Adam's body out of the ground and formed Eve from the bottom of Adam.

I then corrected him, saying Eve wasn't formed from the *"bottom of Adam"* but the "body of Adam." Once he realized what he had said, we laughed hilariously.

On a serious note, one argument against catechism is that kids don't understand what they are parroting back. While this is mostly true for kids aged four to six, I would also argue that this age is when they are the best at memorization. Take advantage of it! Over time, you will have great conversations with your kids about what each question and answer mean. I have seen this in my own family. My son Noah is now fifteen, and we started catechism when he was four. We still talk about what justification and sanctification mean. He didn't get it when he first memorized it, of course, but now he understands these and many other important truths of the faith. It is not uncommon for my older kids to be in the room when I am catechizing Nati, and they hear something and want to have a conversation about it. Think of catechizing like a foundation to build upon over time. A few years ago, while my family was reading through parts of the Old Testament, I decided to make up a chronological chant my kids could memorize in order to have a sketch in their minds of what happened when. This chant is basic and easy; my kids all memorized it when they were about five years old. It only takes kids a few days to get it down.

The Children's Chant: Old Testament Chronology for Three to Five-year-old Children:

Teach each of the Bible stories, then memorize the corresponding saying. You can hear the following chant and its rhythm on my website: http://www.nextgenerationfaithfulness.com/2019/04/03/the-childrens-chant/

Creation
Fall
Flood
Tower of Babel
Abraham
Isaac

Jacob
Joseph
Jacob goes to Egypt with his seventy sons
Moses is saved in a wicker basket
Moses meets God at the burning bush
The water turns to blood
The frogs jumped around
The lice crawled on the people
And the flies flew around
The animals all died and the people got sick
The hail fell down
The locusts flew around
And then it got dark
Death of the firstborn
God parted the Red Sea
God gave the Ten Commandments
The people built the tabernacle
They wandered in the wilderness
Joshua defeated Jericho
The Judges deliver Israel
The United Kingdom of:
Saul
David
Solomon
Rehoboam
The divided Kingdom of Israel and Judah
Israel is destroyed in 722
Judah is destroyed in 586
The Babylonian Exile
Judah returns in 539
The Temple is rebuilt
Esther saves Israel
Nehemiah rebuilds the walls

Worship Through Reading the New Testament: One Year Plan; Eight Years Old and Up; Ten to Fifteen Minutes a Day

The Bible can be tough to understand for a kid. Be patient with your children as you encourage them to become diligent in their reading of the Bible. I developed a small book for kids a few years ago called *New Testament 260*. If you take away weekends, there are 260 solar days (Monday-Friday) in our calendar, and that is the exact number of chapters in the New Testament. A child, adult, or family can read one chapter and memorize one truth from the chapter each weekday and complete the entire New Testament in one year. I used this book for eleven years in a school setting, and it worked out very nicely. Many kids were able to memorize all 260 New Testament truths. At the end of the year, we held a competition to see who had memorized the most. Many parents I know have used it in their homes as well (including myself). All it takes is a commitment to read one chapter a day, five days a week. You can do this with your family. I recommend reading the chapter out loud, but if the children are old enough, let them follow along or do some of the reading. This book can also stand alone and be done by just one person. It comes with of songs to help with memorizing the truths from each chapter. This book can also be found at www. nextgenerationfaithfulness.com.

Worship Through Reading the Whole Bible as a Family; Two Year Plan; Ten Minutes Per Day or Less

Bible Study Together by Peter Schrock guides readers through the entire Bible in two years and comes with maps and other features if you want to utilize them. I highly recommend this work. Schrock has broken down Bible reading into ten-minute daily increments.

Great Books to Buy or Read with Your Eight to Twelve-year-old Children:

Sometimes I take a break from our Bible reading in the morning and read a great story to the kids to start their day. Dave and Neta Jackson wrote a series called *Hero Tales*. These are short stories of people God has used to further the Kingdom through different kinds of mission work. I highly recommend these inspirational stories to start your day. To switch things up one semester, rather than our morning Bible readings, our family read stories from *Hero Tales*. You can read one of these ten-minute stories with a Bible verse and think about what God did through one of his people. They are well-written, and my kids loved them.

For longer reading times or for kids who love to read, Light Keepers Publishing has several books my kids loved including *Ten Boys Who Made a Difference* and *Ten Girls Who Made a Difference*, both by Irene Howat. These short, engaging biographies about some of the most interesting believers in Christian history portray great men and women of God and spur great conversations with your kids.

Heroes of the Faith is another series of biographies kids enjoy, published by Barbour Publishing, Inc. These short books relate the stories of great men and women of God from history.

Voice of the Martyrs puts out the beautifully illustrated *The Kids of Courage* series, which I highly recommend. Your kids will enjoy these books, and they are short enough to use occasionally for family worship time.

We live in an age full of superhero worship. Our kids are inundated with Marvel and DC movies, television shows, and books. Kids dress up like these heroes for Halloween and at home for playtime. I don't think this is a big deal. It's fantasy, and both kids and adults enjoy it. Please, though, do not forget the real hero stories. We should be telling our kids about men and women of God who have done great things for the kingdom of God, people like Hudson Taylor, William Carey, Lottie Moon, Elisabeth Elliot, and a million more just like them. Stories of real-life heroes who lived from the time of the Bible all the way up to today are readily available! Share these with your family!

Themed Readings for Specific Times of the Year:

This past October, my family took a break from our normal Bible reading to read *Martin Luther* by Mike Fearon. This book about Luther's life is published by Bethany House as part of their *Men of Faith* series. My kids really enjoyed reading a chapter a day with me and literally couldn't wait to hear what happened next in the story. We capped off the Reformation series by watching the movie *Luther* on October 31, the actual day Luther nailed The 95 Theses on the castle church door in Wittenberg, Germany in 1517.[8] For our family, October 31st is a night to celebrate Reformation Day. We make some authentic German food together, eat snacks, watch the movie, *Luther*, and talk about the impact of the gospel during Luther's time and our time as well. It is a fun, easy-going family night for us.

We have also read Thanksgiving themed books during the reformation season. In December, we always get our kids Advent calendars. Each day features a Scripture reading, and the kids get a little piece of chocolate from the inside of the calendar. We also read *Come Let us Adore Him* by Paul Tripp during Advent leading up to the birth of Christ. My kids enjoyed the book, but probably enjoyed getting the little piece of chocolate each day just as much. Another good Christmas collection is *Stories Behind the Great Traditions of Christmas* by Ace Collins.

Remember the old saying: "A carpenter is only as good as his tools." There is a plethora of resources available for you to use in the home. If you aren't doing much in terms of family worship, get a game plan together and start working toward faithfulness in this area. If you haven't been doing anything, don't try to bite off too much at once. Work yourself and your family into a faithful pattern of worship at home.

A few ideas on what to watch:

There are several options for watching good biblical works. RightNow Media has incredible resources for families. It's like Netflix for Christians with literally thousands of movies and Bible studies for kids of all ages, as well for as adults. There is a monthly charge for this resource, but it is totally worth the money! I highly recommend checking out this resource which also includes great parenting resources, lectures for moms and dads, and streaming videos that are faithful to the biblical story for both children and adults.

Bible Stories for Kids are well done animated movies faithful to the biblical text. After reading the Bible stories with your kids, you can use these movies to drive home the details. Watching a couple of these movies with your kids on a Friday night is a wonderful way to reinforce the Bible readings you did during the week. But, don't let the movies make you lazy. Keep reading the Word with your children.

I also highly recommend The Bible Project videos. These can and should be watched with all your kids ages ten to eighteen. An illustrator draws the story as a narrator speaks, summarizing entire books of the Bible to help viewers better understand the big picture and purpose of each book. They are instructive and theologically solid as well as enjoyable. These videos always lead to good conversation.

Think of media as a supplement to help spur good Bible conversations.

DON'T GIVE UP

A few years ago, I decided to run a half-marathon for my thirty-fifth birthday. I had never run more than five miles at one time, so I had no experience with long distance running. I decided to run with a friend who was a former cross-country runner and had run several marathons. I consulted him, and we began running together to prepare for my first "half." He became my training partner, and he pushed me.

In order to be ready for the fall run, I had to eat differently, stay consistent during the week in my maintenance run, keep a log, and, once a week, practice the long run with my training partner. Knowing I had to complete a long run with him once a week was built in accountability. He knew every Sunday night whether or not I had cheated that week. Faithfulness was a must as I prepared for a 13.1-mile, non-stop run. I set a goal of running it in two hours flat. When the day finally came, I was totally prepared. My training partner set the pace for each mile as we began the race. When it was over, I finished with a 1:53. The hard work paid off, and I beat my goal by nearly thirty seconds a mile.

I would encourage you to prepare for faithfulness in family worship the same way I prepared for the race. Create achievable short-term goals for yourself with a long-range idea of where you want to end up. If possible, find another family with the same heart and keep each other accountable. If you are faithful, you will most likely exceed your original goals. Remember Paul's charge to Timothy: "Discipline yourself for the purpose of godliness; for bodily discipline is only of little profit, but godliness is profitable for all things, since it holds promise for the present life and also for the life to come" (I Tim. 4:7-8).

Questions to reflect on in this chapter:

1. Will my current priorities allow me to set aside time for family worship?
2. Have I considered what time works well each day (or close to each day) for us to take time and recognize God through reading, singing, and praying?
3. Do I desire to worship God with my family apart from church time? Am I going to get a plan together with my spouse?

Things to remember from this chapter:

1. We are always worshiping something in our home. Family worship is time I specifically set aside in my home to sing, read, and pray with my family.
2. You don't have to have special training to lead your family in worship. Anyone can be faithful to read, sing, and pray with the family.
3. Worship in the home can take many forms when your family comes together. Maybe you need a time of confession. Maybe parents just need to talk about what biblical responsibility looks like for an extended time. Maybe you want to wash each other's feet as a sign of love and humility like Jesus did for his disciples. You can also take time to bless and pray over your children. You can do catechisms or themed readings. The sky is the limit.
4. If you haven't been doing family worship but want to, break your family in slowly. Don't expect to climb Mt. Everest the first day.
5. There are lots of good resources you can watch with your children or allow them to watch on their own, including RightNow Media and The Bible Project videos.
6. Giving up is not an option! I am called to faithfulness.

CHAPTER SIX

SEX & MARRIAGE; SINGLENESS & FRIENDSHIP

Marriage is to be held in honor among all, and the marriage bed is to be undefiled; for fornicators and adulterers God will judge.

Hebrews 13:4

Yet I wish that all men were even as I myself am. However, each man has his own gift from God, one in this manner, and another in that.

1 Corinthians 7:7

David finished talking to Saul. After that, Jonathan became David's closest friend. He loved David as much as he loved himself.

1 Samuel 18:1

SEX AND MARRIAGE

We had some friends and their small children over at our house not too long ago. As the adults began to visit, my attention was quickly drawn to the little children headed for the piano. Then it happened.

My patience for random banging of piano keys lasts roughly two seconds. Why? Because the instrument is not being used as it was intended, thus the sounds from the keys are not in order. The piano requires the key strikes to be orderly. When they are in order, the symmetry leads to beautifully articulated sound. Such symmetry produces works like Mozart's "Moonlight Sonata." When used improperly, the piano can make you want to pull your hair out.

Sex is one of God's greatest gifts to husbands and wives. It is the epitome of human intimacy and expression between couples. It is also an incredibly powerful gift as it allows human beings to join with God in the creation of another human being. Because of this, I encourage you to talk openly about sex with your children. When this gift is exercised in its intended context, God delights in the beauty and symmetry as we would a beautiful piano piece. When sex is engaged in outside of this, it is like the random strikes of piano keys.

Talking with your children about sex and marriage can be intimidating. My advice is that when the time comes, just put your head down and go for it. If you don't, and if you continue to put off "the talk," your kids will learn about it from a friend, the television, or some other type of media. Wouldn't you rather have them learn about it from you?

The first part of this section is called "Sex, Marriage" for the simple reason that within the Christian worldview sex never stands alone. It is an activity only to be expressed through the institution of marriage. To have the "sex talk" apart from the "marriage talk" may disconnect the two ideas for your children. Andy Crouch says in his book, *The Tech Wise Family*, "With sex dissociated so completely from the family, it is perhaps not surprising that family itself, so totally the opposite of easy-everywhere life, is being reconfigured. One in three children in the United States lives without the biological father at home."[1] Again, as the piano keys struck in the right order produce beauty, talking about sex within the context of marriage creates beautiful music. Moms and dads need to lead in this important conversation. Consider that in the public schools today, the "sex talk" is completely disconnected from the "marriage talk."

Nancy Pearcey, professor at Houston Baptist University and author of *Love thy Body: Answering Hard Questions about Life and Sexuality*, recently wrote about this phenomenon:

> Before reaching campus, students are primed by high school sex education courses that typically focus on the physical: on the mechanics of sex and the avoidance of disease and pregnancy. These courses reduce the meaning of sex to a how-to manual. Many students even say the programs make them feel pressured into having sex.[2]

Because this disconnect of sex and marriage exists so prevalently in our culture, Christian parents must guide the ship. Our children must be taught that the commitment of marriage comes before sex, babies, and living together — not after. If a pianist hits a key out of place in "Moonlight Sonata" everyone knows it, but everyone forgets it. If our children hit a "note" out of order in the context of marriage and sex, the possible repercussions and difficulties can be felt for generations. There is grace, mercy, and forgiveness for mistakes, but if you are reading this, I bet you hope your child won't make these mistakes. To help them, talk about this correct "order."

Also, make sure your child knows that no question is off limits. Sex is not dirty. Sex is a wonderful gift from our Creator only to be exercised within the context of marriage (Heb. 13:4). Because God has limited it to the marriage relationship, we should never treat sex in a cavalier manner. Our culture influences children and teenagers to think of sex as "just sex" — something disconnected from relationships. Christians do not have this option. People are sold as property for "just sex." People are murdered for "just sex." A man or woman may risk their vocation or family for "just sex." For us, to indulge in sexual intimacy with husband or wife should be treated as sacred, holy, and beautiful.

WHEN IS MY CHILD OLD ENOUGH TO HAVE "THE TALK?"

The timing is really up to the parent. In *The Hiding Place*, Corrie Ten Boom tells a story about remembering the words "sex sin" being used in a poem she had read. She wanted to know what it meant and asked her mother. Her mother "turned scarlet" and refused to give her an answer. Later, on a train ride with her father, Corrie asked him about "sex sin." What he said next was profound:

> He turned to look at me, as he always did when answering a question, but to my surprise he said nothing. At last he stood up, lifted his traveling case from the rack over our heads, and set it on the floor.
>
> "Will you carry it off the train, Corrie?" he said. I stood up and tugged at it. It was crammed with the watches and spare parts he had purchased that morning.
>
> "It's too heavy," I said.
>
> "Yes," he said. "And it would be a pretty poor father who would ask his little girl to carry such a load. It's the same way, Corrie, with knowledge. Some knowledge is too heavy for children. When you are older and stronger you can bear it. For now, you must trust me to carry it for you."[3]

While this statement exudes wisdom and parents need to be careful not to enter into dialogue too early, I will also say we do not have the luxury of waiting as people in previous times did. With the internet and kids packing around iPhones, your child's potential to see disturbing sexual images at a young age is very high. I know some parents wait until their children go through puberty to begin telling them about sex. They believe once children reach sexual maturity, it will be more natural to teach them about sex. This is a good argument and, again, the decision is up to the parent.

The downside I see to this is that many preteens are resistant to having the talk, possibly because they have reached sexual maturity and feel weird talking about it with their parents. It could also be weird for them because they know more than their parents think.

They may have picked up quite a bit of information on the streets. If this is the case, you should still walk them through it all carefully.

My wife and I decided to have the sex talk with our kids earlier rather than later. We began talking about sex in small bits at around ages nine to ten. We even explained the mechanics. One daughter broke out in hilarious laughter that lasted about twenty minutes (I will never forget that). We kept it somewhat lighthearted, and the kids were inquisitive and unafraid to ask questions, which is what Amy and I wanted. We wanted them to feel natural about the conversation with us, and that's why we were proactive in having the conversations early.

The downside to my approach is that kids may not totally understand the content. When we could tell the kids weren't getting something, we asked them to wait and come back to us later when we would have more time to talk about it. (And they have!) We told them these discussions were off limits with anyone else, but they could ask us anything as they got older. We would explain it, and it was no big deal.

Be thoughtful about the age you decide is right for your children. If your children have friends at school or cousins who are raised in families with different worldviews, you may need to speak to them earlier. Something as sacred and powerful as sex should be taught by the parents. I would also encourage parents to answer any questions their children may have when the talk happens. Shame and fear lead to sin. Don't try to scare your children with statistics of unwanted pregnancies and abortions. This might take away from the beauty of sex within biblical parameters. When the time is right, you might introduce some science, including appropriate pictures for a full explanation of the process. Also, don't forget the details of the stages of baby growth from the sperm attaching to the egg forward. This process is truly incredible!

TALK ABOUT SEX IN A POSITIVE WAY

After many years of ministry and counseling, I have met with many newly married couples struggling to enjoy sex. In my own marriage,

my wife struggled with the transition from twenty-one years of abstinence and guarding her purity to indulging in sex within our
marriage. The "true love waits" movement has done many good
things for the Church by encouraging abstinence, but where is the
teaching in the Church about married couples biblically indulging
in sex? If your children feel they must be in sex-protection mode
their whole lives, they may feel dirty after the consummation of
their marriage. Many new married couples struggle with shame over
sex that is not shameful at all.

After God created Eve, the Bible expounds upon their relationship: "For this reason a man shall leave his father and his mother
and be joined to his wife; and they shall become one flesh. And the
man and his wife were both naked and were not ashamed" (Gen.
2:24-25). Notice that the two "become one flesh." There is a sexual
relationship that is natural between the first couple. We also see that
the man and wife were both "naked and were not ashamed." I
believe the prep work for this one flesh, naked-yet-unashamed experience can be helped along by healthy conversations between
parents and their children. Children should be taught that a
husband and wife in harmony belong to each other. Paul says it this
way: "The wife does not have authority over her own body, but the
husband does; and likewise also the husband does not have
authority over his own body, but the wife does" (1 Cor. 7:4). Children should not be taught to be afraid of sex but rather to respect it.

THE BLESSING OF SINGLENESS

Yes, you read that right. The blessing of singleness. Marriage is not
the end-all of the Christian life. In his book, *Holy Sexuality and the
Gospel*, Christopher Yuan makes the point that the church largely
ignores the goodness of singleness. He says, "Even our unspoken
requirement for pastors to be married means that Jesus and Paul
would be precluded from serving in the vast majority of evangelical
churches today. This should concern us. In our vigorous defends of
traditional marriage, have we misunderstood, undervalued, and
distorted singleness?"[4] Many, including our Savior have led godly

single lives that should inspire us. Marriage is not the end-all, nor is it a cure for loneliness. Think about it. I bet some of the loneliest people you have ever met are married. Since some of our children may grow up to be single, we must briefly look at what the scriptures and history tell us about good godly examples. Healthy single relationships should be part of relationship conversations with our children.

Singleness can be a tremendous blessing from God. Paul said, "I wish that all men were even as I myself am" (1 Cor. 7:7). Paul was talking about being single. He even continued on to encourage widows to remain unmarried unless they were burning with passions (1 Cor. 7:8-9). The blessing of singleness can allow for service to God and others without the normal restraints that come with a healthy marriage. Paul also said, "One who is unmarried is concerned about the things of the Lord, how he may please the Lord; but one who is married is concerned about the things of the world, how he may please his wife, and his interests are divided" (1 Cor. 7:32-34a). The undivided interests of God's people can lead to great things for his kingdom.

The story of Amy Carmichael, who was a great missionary to India, demonstrates the power of a single life devoted to God. She saved countless young children from serving as sex slaves in the temples of India. Carmichael served fifty-five years without a furlough. She was a strong, dedicated single woman, living for the gospel.[5] Lottie Moon also was a single woman and a Baptist missionary to China whose fearless nature and trust in God helped ban the feet binding of women in China. She also reached countless others with the gospel.[6]

Singleness is a beautiful gift of God which he calls some of our children to. Jesus says, "… there are also eunuchs who made themselves eunuchs for the sake of the kingdom of heaven" (Matt. 19:12b). Most interpreters believe Jesus is talking about men who would, like the apostle Paul, commit to living a celibate life so they might advance the gospel. You might be thinking that God said after he created Adam, "It's not good for man to be alone." This is true, but in the larger context of Scripture outside of the marriage context, it can be good for men and women to remain single.

God has created us to become a part of the body which is the Church (Eph. 5:30). Within this body, we should never be lonely. In 1 Corinthians 12, Paul uses the imagery of a body to describe the Church. This demonstrates the interconnectedness of every member to the rest and of the whole to Christ, who is our head. Paul lived a celibate life with great friends such as Luke, Timothy, and Silas. His great friendship with the elders of Miletus can be seen in Acts 20 as they weep over Paul who is leaving them. Being single does not equal being lonely. It can be a true blessing from the Lord and should be celebrated.

FRIENDSHIP WITH THE WORLD IS NOT FRIENDSHIP WITH UNBELIEVERS

1 John 2:15 tells us we should not "love the world or the things in the world." James 4:4 says that "friendship with the world is hostility toward God." Do these verses imply we should refrain from friendships with unbelievers? Not at all! In fact, Paul says in 1 Corinthians 5:9-10, "I wrote you in my letter not to associate with immoral people; I did not at all mean with the immoral people of this world, or with the covetous and swindlers, or with idolaters, for then you would have to go out of the world." Paul makes it clear that we are to associate with immoral people because the gospel is for them! Paul warns against associating with people who claim to be believers but live a life of consistent sin without repentance. So, what were John and James talking about then? They were talking about loving worldly things and adopting the world's values rather than putting God first.

1 Peter 2:11 tells us we are "foreigners and exiles." This world is not our home. If we dig in here on earth and spend all our time, money, and resources on worldly pleasures, we aren't living as foreigners and exiles. Jesus says, "Where your treasure is, there your heart will be also" (Matt. 6:21). We don't love the world, but we are to love lost people. Taking Jesus as our example, Romans 5:8 says,

"But God demonstrates his own love toward us, in that while we were yet sinners, Christ died for us." Jesus loved us while we were still sinners, not yet covered by his grace. Teach your children that their lost friends at school and in the neighborhood need to be shown the love of Christ. They should befriend these lost children.

Christian parents, this doesn't mean you should just cut your children loose to associate with everyone. Use discretion and wisdom. 1 Corinthians 15:33 says, "Bad company corrupts good morals." Some of their lost friends should probably only be in a controlled environment with them, maybe with you at the helm. In a controlled situation, your children can be a good friend to unbelievers.

On the old television show, *Leave It to Beaver*, there was a character named Eddie Haskell. Eddie was the kid who was always very respectful when the adults were around. When they turned their heads, he was the first to come up with an ornery plan. Eddie played the system. Teach your children to be careful with the Eddie Haskells and to avoid becoming one themselves. Friends whose parents are teaching them a Christian worldview might be okay in almost any situation. However, don't assume anything, and help your children to be wise in all their friendships. If an unbeliever has too much influence on them, make sure you monitor the situation.

Pray with your children about their friends who are unbelievers, and help your children know that as a young Christian, they have a responsibility to bring the light of the gospel into that friendship. Remember Jesus' parable about the good shepherd who left the ninety-nine to fetch the one lost sheep (Luke 15:3-7). Jesus is that good shepherd. Our kids shouldn't be only hanging out in Christian cliques. They, just like us, should have the heart of Jesus who came to "seek and to save the lost" (Luke 19:10). Colossians 4:5-6 says, "Conduct yourselves with wisdom toward outsiders, making the most of the opportunity. Let your speech always be with grace, as though seasoned with salt, so that you will know how you should respond to each person."

When my wife and I were newly married and I was serving at my first church, we befriended a young couple named Michael and

Mischelle. We instantly hit it off with them and began hanging out together. Michael was pretty rough with his language at the time, and neither of them had much church background. Michael would always say what was on his mind, and at times, it would make Amy and me uncomfortable. We prayed for Michael and Mischelle consistently. Eventually, that rough exterior began to fade away. Both of them came to faith in the gospel and were baptized at our church. Both served in the youth ministry with us and eventually Michael felt the call to full-time ministry. Eighteen years later, Michael and Mischelle are serving at their first full-time church. I always remind myself of Michael and Mischelle when I'm around someone who seems like they have no hope. You never know what our amazing God will do.

CHRISTIAN FRIENDSHIPS

A Christian friendship can be one of the most beautiful blessings of the Christian life. I have some tremendous friends who care deeply about my life and walk with Jesus. Some of them would do almost anything for me, and I would do anything for them as well. But friendships can be difficult. Help your children navigate the difficult waters of conflict, gossip, and drama. Walk them carefully through what the scriptures say about these things as they

grow in their sanctification. Matthew 18:15-17 is a great place to start during conflict.

Encourage your children to get to the other side of these situations without losing their temper or their friend. Relationships are critical, and during their formative years, your child will need to learn how to deal with conflict resolution in friendship. Make sure you are handling your own friendships with integrity. Don't just be a hearer and herald of the Word. Be a doer of the Word. Your children will watch your example and learn how to have friendships. By God's grace, I have had many Christian friends through the years who have helped me love God more. They have challenged me when I was in error, encouraged me when I was down, and rejoiced with me when something went well.

The friendship of David and Jonathan in the Old Testament is a great example of sacrificial love between friends. Jonathan is said to have loved David as much as he loved himself. Jonathan was even willing to give up the familial bond of the father-son relationship with King Saul to help save his friend (1 Sam. 20). Friendships like these last because each person cares about the other's feelings and needs as much as they care about their own.

Paul and Timothy are another great example of a special friendship. Paul calls Timothy in 1 Timothy 1:2 "[his] true son in the faith." Paul says in Philippians 2:3-4, "Do nothing from selfishness or empty conceit, but with humility of mind regard one another as more important than yourselves; do not merely look out for your own personal interests, but also for the interests of others." When we have a deep commitment to friendship in the Church and elsewhere, we see the love of Jesus Christ.

The problem Paul dealt with in Philippi when he wrote these words was division within the body of Christ. He called Euodia and Syntyche to live in harmony (Phil. 4:2). Apparently, the infighting had reached such a level in the Philippian church that Paul had to call these women out while he was imprisoned in Rome. This is not the mind of Christ. Psalm 133:1 says, "Behold, how good and how pleasant it is for brothers to dwell together in unity."

If your children have friendships with other children who love the Lord, encourage them to pray together, worship together, and do missions together. Get together with believing families for nights of family worship. Make sure to foster the spiritual growth of these friendships, providing not just a way for them to hang out but a way for them to connect over the gospel. Singing songs, reading the Bible, or just talking about the Lord with your children and their Christian friends encourages their relationships to grow in the Lord.

Questions to reflect on in this chapter:

1. Am I ready to begin having sex and marriage talks with my child, about both the mechanics and the meaning behind it all?

2. Have I approached sex as a standalone topic or explained it within the context of marriage?

3. Am I mentally prepared to talk about sex in a positive light with my children?

4. Have I thought about the possibility that my child may be single their whole life? Am I prepared to talk to them about the blessing a single life can be?

5. Am I prepared to talk to my children about the difference between friends who are non-Christian and friends who are Christian? Do I monitor carefully my children's friendships?

Things to remember from this chapter:

1. The age to share information about marriage and sex with a child is up to the parent. There is obviously an age that is too young; however, you don't want them learning it on the streets, either.

2. The sex talk should always be connected to the marriage talk for Christians. These aren't standalone issues for us.

3. Sex always leaves open the chance that a baby made in the image of God will be born. Man is too important to create thoughtlessly.

4. Some of the loneliest people in the world are married. Marriage is not the cure for loneliness.

5. When friends live sacrificially toward one another, we see a picture of the gospel.

CHAPTER SEVEN

KINGDOM BUILDING: NOT JUST FOR ADULTS

Let no one look down on your youthfulness, but rather in speech, conduct love, faith and purity, show yourself an example of those who believe.

I Timothy 4:12

"You may speak but a word to a child, and in that child there may be slumbering a noble heart which shall stir the Christian Church in years to come."[1]

C.H. Spurgeon

DON'T COUNT OUT THE YOUNG

You may have first heard "Allegri's Miserere" in the movie *Chariots of Fire*. It's the kind of music that, once heard, can't easily be forgotten. It was originally transcribed and hidden within the Vatican around 1630. This beautiful piece of music was only played in the Sistine Chapel on the Wednesday and Friday of Holy Week. Its release was strictly forbidden, and anyone caught with it was excommunicated from the church.

140 years later, a fourteen-year-old boy traveled to Rome with

his father to experience Holy Week. On Wednesday, they visited the Sistine Chapel and heard the beautiful "Allegri's Miserere." That night the boy had trouble sleeping in the small bed with his father, so he left the bed, sat down, and transcribed the piece from memory — perfectly! Soon, the piece was printed and quickly spread throughout Europe.

The next year, The Vatican summoned the boy to meet with Pope Clement XIV. Instead of excommunicating the boy, Clement praised him for his musical genius.[2] After 140 years, the ban was lifted. The music could legally be shared!

You might know this boy from history as Wolfgang Amadeus Mozart. Obviously, Mozart was a special kind of talent whose genius is seen maybe once in a century, but don't forget we serve a God who always does the unexpected. "God has chosen the foolish things of the world to shame the wise, and God has chosen the weak things of the world to shame the things which are strong" (1 Cor. 1:27).

Consider the story of missionary Brian Hogan who moved to Mongolia to spread the gospel in the early 1990s. There was nearly no gospel presence in Mongolia before Hogan and his family arrived. At first, they saw few results, but then the gospel began to take root in the lives of fourteen teenage girls. These fourteen girls were the first converts in their city of Erdenet. Amazingly, God used these young girls to start a gospel movement as thousands came to Christ in the next few years. You can read his story in his book, *There's a Sheep in My Bathtub.*[3]

God can certainly use the young to do amazing things.

HOW OLD WERE THE DISCIPLES?

Many believe Jesus' disciples may have been only teenagers. The argument typically refers to a particular passage in the Gospel of Matthew when a dispute arose about whether or not Jesus should pay taxes. In the larger context of this passage, all the disciples were traveling together, but the discourse was only between Jesus and Peter. Here is the text:

When they came to Capernaum, those who collected the two-drachma tax came to Peter and said, "Does your teacher not pay the two-drachma tax?" He said, "Yes." And when he came into the house, Jesus spoke to him first, saying, "What do you think, Simon? From whom do the kings of the earth collect customs or poll-tax, from their sons or from strangers?" When Peter said, "From strangers," Jesus said to him, "Then the sons are exempt. However, so that we do not offend them, go to the sea and throw in a hook, and take the first fish that comes up; and when you open its mouth, you will find a shekel. Take that and give it to them for you and me."

Matthew 17:25-27

Notice that Jesus tells Peter when he opens the mouth of the fish he will find a shekel that will pay the tax for both of them. This tax was originally given by the Jews for the upkeep of the tabernacle in the Old Testament as prescribed in Exodus 30:11-14. During Jesus' day, males aged twenty to fifty continued to pay this tax for the upkeep of the Temple.[4] When Jesus tells Peter to take the money from the fish's mouth, it is just for him and Peter. Jesus doesn't say anything about paying for the other disciples. Many believe that since the only two persons paying the tax are Jesus and Peter, the rest must have been teenagers. Even if they weren't, the disciples were very young. The only known disciple to have been married during the time of Jesus was Peter (1 Cor. 9:5). If it is true that the disciples were just teenagers, it is more compelling evidence that God uses young people for great things.

However old they were, God used their preaching of the gospel to turn the world upside down. Encourage your children and teens to be faithful to God's calling on their lives and to let "no one look down on [their] youthfulness." Today we believe our children must finish high school and go to college or trade school before they can really be impactful in our culture. What would Jesus think of this? Have we perhaps shortchanged our children by not activating them at a younger age to serve the living God with zeal? Imagine how many times the disciples must have messed up when they were following Jesus from town to town. He, the Rabbi, remained incredibly patient with them throughout this process of growth. His healings contained object lessons (Luke 17:11-19), his miracles challenged their faith (Mark 4:39-40), his acceptance of the unclean blew their minds (John 4:7-27), and his teaching about who was the greatest humbled them greatly (Luke 22:24-27). These young men were exposed to a myriad of situations and forced to live out their Christian worldview. Do we provide these opportunities for our children?

FIVE NEEDLES UNDER A HAYSTACK

Samuel J. Mills, James Richards, Francis L. Robbins, Harvey Loomis, and Byram Green were all students at Williams College in 1806. These five friends often discussed theological issues. One particular day while outside near a river, they were suddenly caught in a brief thunderstorm and forced to take refuge under a haystack. The topic of discussion became their concern for the spiritually lost countries around the world. From that seemingly insignificant and strange prayer meeting under the haystack, these five young men founded the American Board of Commissioners for Foreign Missionaries (ABCFM). Although these men faced ridicule from their classmates, they remained devoted to Christ and fervent in their prayer.[5] Samuel Mills "exhorted his companions with the words that later became a watchword for them: We can do this if we will."[6]

In 1812, the ABCFM sent out its first five missionaries including Adoniram Judson and Luther Rice.[7] Because God laid a vision in the heart of these young men under the haystack, their faithfulness in commissioning men and women to do gospel work became a needle in the side of Satan. In the twentieth century, the organization merged with the United Church of Christ. However, its initial work was one of faithful gospel proclamation to the nations.

Again, God uses the young for great things! Do your children belong to a group of friends their age that pray together? Maybe you can help them start one. Are you encouraging or actively involved in mission trips with your children? In 2018, my wife and I had the opportunity to take our eleven and twelve-year-old daughters on an international mission trip to Zambia in Africa. We challenged them to journal each day of the experience to both remember details and also write down how God was using it to change their lives. The experience was truly a game-changer for them. Their introduction to poverty on that scale broke their hearts for both the physical and spiritual condition of the lost. They were also both instrumental in helping lead a VBS in a Christian school for poor children. The experience challenged them to share their faith and to love those who have been forgotten by the world. Please encourage your children to dream big for the kingdom of God and get them involved. They can and will make a difference.

HAVE AN ACTS 1:8 VISION FOR YOUR CHILDREN

What is the last thing you say to your family before walking out the door to go to work or on a trip? I always tell them I love them, and I bet you do, too. Why do we do that? We do it because if something were to happen to us or them, that is what we want remembered. We loved each other. When we look at Jesus' last words to his disciples, I can't help but think the same thing was in his mind for the Church. His last words should be incredibly meaningful and powerful for all believers: "But you will receive power when the Holy Spirit has come upon you; and you shall be my witnesses both in Jerusalem, and in all Judea and Samaria, and even to the remotest part of the earth" (Acts 1:8). When you look carefully at the end of each of the Gospels, Jesus, just as in this passage, gives the Great Commission. All four Gospels record it, each in a different setting. So, taken along with this passage from the book of Acts, it is safe to say Jesus not only gave the Great Commission to his disciples in the resurrection at least five times but that it was also his last words to the Church!

It always amazes me when I see cults with a better discipling game plan than the Church. Every year, young Mormon boys and girls in grades nine through twelve rise early in the morning to attend "seminary." Here, before school, they learn what they believe and how to articulate that to prepare for their two-year mission after graduation. These kids will travel way out of their comfort zones while they are on mission. You have probably seen these young men and women bicycling or driving around two by two to share the Mormon faith in your town. These young people are brought up in a system that helps them look forward to a proactive sharing of their faith. When my wife and I come across them in our community, we always invite them in and ask them where they are from. Many times, they are over a thousand miles away from home on their mission. Amy and I have fed Mormon missionary kids dinner more than once to build relationships with them and tell them the gospel.

Why does the Church not have that same vision for our young people? Why are we not as zealous as they? We have the truth of the gospel; they have an imitation. A simple plan of action for us might be to look again at the Great Commission and use it as the catalyst for missions involvement for our children. Jesus says in Acts 1:8, "You shall be witnesses to me in Jerusalem, and in all Judea and Samaria, and to the end of the earth."

Jerusalem is where the disciples were when they received this command from Jesus. In other words, Jesus is saying to start right where you are at. Get involved in a domestic mission project through your church such as a project that helps feed the hungry. Volunteer at a homeless shelter. Use these missions as a platform to preach the gospel. Going to "Jerusalem" is getting involved in our own backyards.

When Christ mentions Judea and Samaria, he is stretching the circle. Judea was to the south while Samaria was to the north. As your children get older, show them the needs of other communities by going on mission outside of your city and state. This can demonstrate that the need for the gospel and for the love of Christ is not just at home but all around them.

Finally, Jesus says to go "to the ends of the earth." Save money along with your children to go on an international trip before they leave the home. Expose them to the need of the gospel on an international scale. The Joshua Project currently estimates that 41%

of the world is still unreached with the gospel! Each family should do their part to go on mission in their own Jerusalem, Judea, Samaria, and to the ends of the earth.

If you don't like the above plan, create one of your own. The key is intentionality, working toward something. When your children come to faith in the gospel, sit down with them and develop a plan of faithfulness for using their gifts within the Church to further the kingdom of God. The quicker you can integrate them into service and action, the quicker they will move from consumer to giver. We need to seriously ask ourselves if the Mormons are more faithful to their religion than we are to ours.

WORK OF HEART (ONE KID'S JERUSALEM)

Whenever your child has something on his heart that he wants to do for God or others, if you are able to facilitate it, please do. In 2016 in West Plains, Missouri, a twelve-year-old girl had a heart for the poor of Africa and China. Kelly wanted to help others. She knew I had started a school for orphans and impoverished children in Africa, and ever since third grade, she had saved her milk money and brought it to me to use for those kids. After making sure this was okay with her parents, I took that money and gave it to the work of the school.

When Kelly was in seventh grade, she wanted to do something bigger. She asked God to show her how she could do something for an orphanage in China and a Christian school in Africa. After prayer and talking with her parents, she decided to challenge her classmates to help with a fundraiser. Her parents weren't sure about her idea, but because they knew she had a heart for missions, and they did, too, they didn't want to squelch her heart.

Kelly challenged students from kindergarten through high school to create pieces of artwork to sell at an art fair. Her parents and I believed God was moving her heart to do this, so we told her to go for it. Kelly decided to name her idea "Work of heART." She shared her idea with her classmates and school, and they quickly jumped on board. Over eighty students created 123 art pieces over the next month! A local business hosted the event, and the place was packed! Kelly's initial goal was to raise $500. All the artwork sold, a generous donor matched the final total, and Kelly's "Work of heART" raised $4,321.42! That money went to feed very poor children and also to expose them to the life-changing message of Jesus! 1 Timothy 4:12 says, "Let no one look down on your youthfulness, but rather in speech, conduct, love, faith and purity, show yourself an example of those who believe."

Do you encourage your children to do great things for the kingdom of God?

PLAYING WITH FIRE

"One day, you're gonna set the world on fire," Mrs. Aiken, my second-grade teacher, told me. I was scared to death of what she meant. My mother still tells the story about how I came home and promised her I hadn't been playing with matches. When she asked why I was telling her that, I repeated what Mrs. Aiken had said. My mother looked at me and said, "Well, you are." I wanted to cry until she explained it in a way I could understand. According to my mom, Mrs. Aiken had given me a huge compliment.

Mom and Mrs. Aiken were two of my earliest fans. They both believed that, although I was ornery at the time, God had something big in store for me. My mom was always telling me God had a plan for my life and that he was going to use me. I remember her saying that and feeling as if it was true, as if I could do something great for God. She often reminded me that whether something went well or poorly, it was "all part of the plan" God had for my life.

Believing her words to be true, I have tried to live my life in such a way that it would have an impact on the kingdom. My mom was my cheerleader, and I try to do the same for my kids. Are you reminding your children of the big purpose God has in store for their lives? Are you growing within them the sense of calling and responsibility "to love God and enjoy him forever?" As we determine to faithfully hand down the truth of our faith to our kids through the teaching of the Word, we should also seek to hand down a sense of calling on their individual lives. As they come to faith in the gospel, help them discover and use their spiritual gifts for God's kingdom.

Paul gives the list of spiritual gifts in three places: Ephesians 4:11, 1 Corinthians 12, and Romans 12. Look carefully at those gifts mentioned and try to discern which are emerging in your children as they grow toward maturity. Maybe your child is very generous. Many times, parents will tell their kids to not give away their things. This could be the spiritual gift of generosity beginning to bloom (Rom. 12:8). Maybe your child is naturally a servant (1 Cor. 12:7) or very merciful toward others (1 Cor. 12:8). If they are born-again and you see special things about their personalities, don't chalk those things up to mere genetics. It could be that those are spiritual gifts in their embryonic stages that God wants to bring to maturity in them to change the world! A parent has the inside track into how their kids are wired. Recognize their spiritual gifts and help them see how to use those to further the kingdom of God.

A BOOK, THE GOSPELS, A PRAYER, A TRIP, AN ENCOURAGING MOM

In 2009, I felt a deep stirring to help the poor and vulnerable be filled and hear the gospel. I read *The Hole in our Gospel* by Richard Stearns, President of World Vision. In this book, he talks about how little money the American church spends on foreign missions. He also details the latest statistics on how many children in impoverished countries die daily from preventable diseases and causes. After finishing, I went back to the Gospels and re-read them carefully. One parable of Jesus really stuck with me:

> The land of a rich man was very productive. And he began reasoning to himself, saying, "What shall I do, since I have no place to store my crops?" Then he said, "This is what I will do: I will tear down my barns and build larger ones, and there I will store all my grain and my goods. And I will say to my soul, Soul, you have many goods laid up for many years to come; take your

ease, eat, drink and be merry." But God said to him, "You Fool! This very night your soul is required of you; and now who will own what you have prepared?" So is the man who stores up treasure for himself, and is not rich toward God.

    Luke 12:13-21

That passage reminded me of American culture. The guy in the parable is a typical American who would be deemed a good planner. However, in the context of first century culture where people who had clothes, shelter, and food for the day were considered rich, this man was greedy. I didn't want to be greedy with any of my resources. If I could help people, I really wanted to.

In December of 2009, a friend and I hit our knees before God and begged him to help us be faithful to take the gospel to the nations. It was an emotional prayer time when both of us were under the convicting power of the Spirit. When we finished praying, a name came to my mind — Victor Chibangula. I hadn't talked with Victor for four years. He was a church planter friend I met in seminary in 2004. After reconnecting with him through email, he invited me to visit him and talk about possible ministry work.

My friend and I boarded a plane in July of 2010 to look into ministry with Victor in Zambia. As we all prayed together, it became apparent that God was going to work through us to begin a ministry. When we traveled to a poor, forgotten village with no presence of the gospel, our hearts were broken. We fed some children and villagers and gave them some clothing. As a church planting strategy, we decided to start a Christian school where the gospel could be clearly proclaimed to the children each day. We would also feed the children a nutrient-filled meal each day (something none of them had at the time).

We left this desperately poor village community with hungry children knowing we had to follow through with our plan. However, once I boarded the plane, doubt began to creep into my mind. I reasoned with myself about being too busy, about not having the money, resources, or know-how to start a school in Africa. The longer the plane ride, the more I doubted. By the time we landed in Washington, D.C., I had nearly talked myself out of doing anything.

Then, I called my mom. As I told her about the trip and the poor children, I heard her emotionally moved on the other end of the phone. I told her about a five-year-old boy named Gift — how both of his parents were dead and how he walked around barefoot and hungry. Then I paused and said, "I think it's too big. I'm not sure we can really make a difference. I don't know if anyone will give, and I'm having serious doubts this will ever get off the ground." A few seconds later she said, "I'll help Gift. I will give to those children. You have to do something for those kids, and I want to be the first one to give. You can do this!"

That conversation took place nine years ago. As of 2019, by God's grace and through generous donors like my mother who have a heart for the poor to be fed and hear the gospel, we now have two Bethlehem Christian Academy campuses in Zambia and one in the 10/40 window of West Africa. Over three hundred students eat a good meal every day and receive a Christian education. Several have come to faith in the gospel, and Gift Bwepe is now in the fifth grade. BCA has multiple partner churches in Missouri and Arkansas and over five hundred monthly givers. It continues to expand and will soon have a high school at each campus.

Do you believe and encourage your kids to do great things for the kingdom? My mom is still my biggest fan. Encourage your kids to take risks for the one who gave his all for us on the cross.

Questions to reflect on in this chapter:

1. Have I been faithful to look for opportunities for my children to help build God's kingdom?
2. Have I believed that it always takes more seasoned people to make a difference in the spreading of the gospel?
3. Do I have a vision for my kids to fulfill Acts 1:8 after they have come to faith?

4. Have I been a cheerleader for my kids to do things for Jesus?

Things to remember from this chapter:

1. God used a group of teenage girls to move the gospel in Mongolia.
2. Even if the disciples weren't teenagers, they were young when God used them to shake up the world.
3. Even a twelve-year-old girl can follow through on a big vision for the Lord.
4. Moms and dads are critical in cheering on their kids to do great things for the Lord.

CHAPTER EIGHT

THE INTERNET: KEEP HOPE IN THE BOX

Can a man take fire in his bosom and his clothes not be burned?
  Proverbs 6:27

I am convinced that pervasive Internet pornography has become the greatest barrier to faith in Christ, and we simply must do something about it.[1]
  Josh McDowell

THE HOOKS

"BUT THEY'RE A GOOD KID!"

If I had a nickel for every time I heard a parent say that about one of their kids in trouble, I would be a rich man. Oh, I think I know what they are trying to say, and relatively speaking, I get it. I would like to think of my kids as "good kids" as well. The dilemma is that, theologically, all mankind is sinful. Paul says in Romans 3:10, "There is none righteous, not even one…"

I remember a former student whose parents hooked up the internet for him in his room. He was a young, shy kid at the time and never in trouble, affable and obedient in almost every way. He came to me when he was nineteen and told me he was addicted to pornography. Now, by our definition of "good kids," this was a "great kid." This all-American boy came to me, confessing that for years he had been in an intense struggle to overcome his addiction. His mom and dad assumed he would never get involved in something like that. He didn't think he would, either, but one night he accidentally stumbled upon something he shouldn't have, and the hooks were in.

These same hooks dig their way into many young Christian lives without their parents knowing. The shame is too much to bear, so they keep it quiet to avoid disappointing their parents. Maybe they have tried time and time again to overcome the problem but feel helpless, depressed, and alone. This could be *your* child, today or some day in the future. Have you made your home a place where confession, repentance, and restoration are welcome? Do your kids feel you would run to them as did the prodigal son's father? Or might they be afraid of shunning and shaming?

I remember exactly where I was standing the first time I saw pornography. I was around ten years old, helping my friend cut grass at an apartment complex. I was weed-eating a small, secluded section behind the apartment, and as I moved along the edge of some railroad ties, I hit some kind of paper that shot into the air. I put down the weed-eater and looked closer; it was a porn magazine. I don't think I even knew the word porn, but I quickly threw down the magazine and moved on.

Not two minutes later, my curiosity got the best of me, and I wanted to see more. Initially, I was disgusted, but within minutes, I wanted a second look. Little did I know at the time that a gate had opened that needed to be shut quickly. That first encounter was not subtle. I had never encountered any media or anything else that had awakened the unfamiliar emotions I felt. Our culture has radically changed since 1986.

Clothing is a grace from God. I don't just mean on a cold day. I mean that it is actually a picture of the saving grace of God. What did Adam and Eve do as soon as they sinned? After they ate the fruit, Scripture says, "Then the eyes of both of them were opened, and they knew that they were naked; and they sewed fig leaves together and made themselves loin coverings" (Gen. 3:7). The minute sin entered the world, the natural thing Adam and Eve wanted to do was cover their parts. The fig leaf speedo wasn't quite enough. After God spoke with them and handed down the curses, the Bible records, "The Lord God made garments of skin for Adam and his wife, and clothed them" (Gen. 3:21). Because of the gravity of sin, an animal lost its life. This was the first sacrifice for man and woman that we see in the Bible.

Those first garments, made from a dead animal, were not only a physical covering but also a spiritual one. Every time Adam and Eve put them on, the clothing reminded them of the goodness of God's grace. I don't think it is too much to extrapolate that we should dress in such a way that fits the grace bestowed upon our first parents. In other words, we should remember that we dress not only to cover up physical things, but we dress in a way that shows we have a spiritual covering as well.

The first Adam was covered. The second Adam died naked on a cross. That's right, naked. The loincloth you see Jesus wearing in movies wasn't really there. That is a powerful moment in history as we contrast the two Adams. The first Adam, as guilty as he was, received forgiveness and grace and covering from breaking the law. The second Adam, as innocent as he was, received the full wrath of God which belonged to the law breakers. The exposed second Adam died in place of the covered first Adam. "For as through the one man's disobedience the many were made sinners, even so through the obedience of the One the many will be made righteous" (Rom. 5:19). When the people of a culture begin to uncover themselves publicly, they deny the one who was uncovered in their place. Such a culture will steadily move further and further away from the gospel. This is exactly what internet porn is doing to our world.

HAVE WE BECOME DESENSITIZED?

It is a well-established fact that the human mind will accept anything if given enough time to adjust and if accompanied by a rationale that disarms defenses. In the 1930s and 40s, four groups of twenty men moved across Eastern Europe during World War II. These relatively small groups of men were known as Nazi killing squads. They alone murdered about 1.4 million people in cold blood. They spared neither women nor children nor babies. On several occasions, they killed as many as fifty thousand Jews, Gypsies, Poles, and political prisoners in a single day. How could these men have carried out such horrible crimes? You must be thinking they were deranged and out of their minds!

After the war, we learned these men were primarily normal human beings — former businessmen, doctors, lawyers, and shop-keepers.[2] If so, how could they become immune to the horror of murder? The answer? They were systematically desensitized. The book *Ordinary Men* by Christopher Browning recounts the strange fact that some of the cruelest killers in the Nazi regime were next-door-neighbor kind of people. Unexpected cruelty can form in the heart after desensitization. The Nazis had a plan for growing their recruits into hardened killers. "Nazi recruits would be given beau-tiful German shepherd puppies as their own and allowed to become emotionally attached. Then they forced the men to break the necks of the puppies with their bare hands. This was done to make them 'tough' and to desensitize them to cruelty. It is a short distance emotionally from killing cuddly dogs to murdering defenseless human beings."[3]

Desensitization happens slowly, methodically, and over time. Exposure to pornography can lead to addiction. Addiction by nature desensitizes a person. After a person is desensitized, they are capable of more than just looking at porn. It can lead to acting out sexually. The Proverbs warn us over and over again about the pitfalls of immorality. Proverbs 6:27-29 says:

Can a man take fire in his bosom and his clothes not be burned?

Or can a man walk on hot coals and his feet not be scorched? So is the one who goes in to his neighbor's wife; whoever touches her will not go unpunished.

A steady diet of taking that fire into your heart will lead to real problems. Guard yourself and your children. The longer someone stays hooked in, the more erotic and degrading the experience must be to excite the addict. It is a dangerous addiction, and all of us should take precautions to keep ourselves and our children safe.

MANAGING THE BOX

In the year 2000, I drove around in my red, extended-cab Chevy with a bag phone on my console. I felt pretty cool with that phone even though the reception was terrible and it cost too much for me to actually use. There was no way we could have foreseen just how incredibly powerful cell phones would become.

Working in youth ministry during the time cell phone technology boomed, with text messaging and the ability to send pictures, I have many stories of students making poor choices. As the headmaster of a Christian school for eleven years, I watched students time and time again make poor choices with their cellular devices. Is it wise to give a teenager so much power?

Do you know the Greek myth about a girl who had been given clothing from Athena, beauty from Aphrodite, and musical prowess from Apollo himself? Her name was Pandora, and she had a small box that contained all the evils of the world. Pandora opened the box (*pithos*, actually a jar) and let out all the evils into the world. The only thing she was able to trap inside the box was hope.[4]

Kids today carry around little Pandora's boxes. There is incredible potential for your teen to get messed up simply from owning a cell phone. Fifteen-year-old boys and girls barely on the other side of puberty are struggling with sexual self-control. A cell phone provides easy access to the evils of this world. My question for you is, have you, like Pandora, captured "hope" in the box? If your child's cell phone doesn't have excellent protections installed, you have no idea what they are really doing on that phone. According to a recent Barna Group study, 62% of teenagers have received nude images on their phone and 40% have sent one.[5] Fortunately, some very good protections for cell phones and computers are available to families. Unfortunately, most don't stand a chance against a highly motivated, tech savvy teen. You must look into utilizing good tools and technologies to monitor and keep up with your kids' activities.

I highly recommend you read Andy Crouch's *The Tech-Wise Family*, a book with internet device awareness tips for you and your family. Apps and software are available that can help you with safety. We have Covenant Eyes software for all our devices. This report-based software allows your accountability partner to see anything you have viewed. All activity is recorded and available for your partner to sift through. Covenant Eyes also uses a rating system so the task of reviewing websites isn't too laborious, and you can easily spot possible problem sites. Circle with Disney is another good web traffic reviewer. It allows you to shut down any websites you don't want your kids to see and provides a filter level you can turn up or down at any time. It works on all your family's devices and tracks apps as well as websites. You can also set online time limits for your kids. Sometimes our family will take one entire week and have a media fast. No movies, television, iPads, or phones. To be honest, it is quite liberating. We read more, play games more, and talk more. I encourage you to try it if you have never done it. It is a good way to find out if you are in control of media or if it is in control of you. I plead with you parents, if you haven't already done so, get good protections and trap some "hope" in the box.

DON'T TAKE YOUR EYE OFF THE BALL

One morning in my second year of running a Christian school, I finished reading the Bible and praying with students during the daily chapel service. The kids left, following their teachers to the classrooms to begin the day. As I folded and leaned chairs against the wall and unplugged my PowerPoint, I noticed someone at the back of the chapel trying to hide around the corner near the bathroom. I could barely see a leg sticking into the hallway. I barked a little at the kid to go to class, the leg disappeared, and I continued to break down the chapel service. A few minutes later, I saw the leg again near the edge of the door. I walked over to see what was going on and found a student who had had a major pee accident. A third-grade boy had started and apparently couldn't stop. This was complete saturation! The child was already embarrassed, so I told him it was no big deal and to follow me to my office where I could call his mom to bring him some clothes.

As he stood in my office, I quickly walked into the secretary's office and grabbed the phone. When I returned, the kid was sitting in my big, cloth-covered chair! It was soaked. I took my eye off him for a minute, and all was lost. Kids are like that, right? The minute you think you're in the clear, you get a big surprise. If the cell phones and computers in your homes don't have internet filters on them with real accountability, you have taken your eye off the ball, and there is probably a kid sitting in a "mess in your chair." Andy Crouch says in *The Tech Wise Family*, "It is astonishing how many parents blithely give young children smartphones that allow absolutely unfettered access to whatever the internet (and links from their friends) may serve up."[6] I would like to echo this sentiment. Either parents don't really know the dangers or think they have a "good kid" who would never do anything like that.

The truth is that a teen has enough trouble controlling themselves without the power of the world at their fingertips. While I understand that many kids are in fact "good kids," parents must be more astute than that in their child rearing. If you don't have protections on your kids' devices, I encourage you to install some as soon as possible.

SCRIPTURES AND OTHER RESOURCES

The Word of God is full of warnings about lust and sexual sin. Paul says we shouldn't let even a hint of sexual immorality be named among us. God warns us that lies, which come from the father of lies, often disguise themselves as truth and light.

Because so many of us are both visual and impulsive, the internet can lead to some major sin problems. The disciplines and accountability are as crucial as ever for the Spirit to work sanctification in us today. In Proverbs 7, an old father narrates the story of a young man's downfall to warn his own son that the path of lust and adultery leads to destruction. The behavior of the seductress first pulls him in, only to reveal that, in the end, she is a destroyer. "With her flattering lips she seduces him. Suddenly he follows her as an ox goes to the slaughter, or as one in fetters to the discipline of a fool..." (Prov. 7:21-22). This passage is a powerful warning that although the moment may be exciting, the situation leads to destruction.

> My son, keep my words and treasure my commandments within you. Keep my commandments and live, and my teaching as the apple of your eye. Bind them on your fingers; write them on the tablet of your heart. Say to wisdom, 'You are my sister,' and call understanding your intimate friend; at that they may keep you from an adulteress, from the foreigner who flatters with her words.
> Proverbs 7:1-4

Not only am I reading Scriptures like this with my teenage son, but I'm also reading books such as *Every Young Man's Battle*, by Stephen Arterburn and Fred Stoeker. These guys tell their stories of encountering pornography, the destructive path it took them down, and how God liberated them from the chains of addiction. As I read these stories with my son, I am thankful to God that I get a chance to warn him with good council from the Word of God and with the testimony of men who have worked hard to put the sin of porn to death in their own lives.

As your girls and boys become preteens and teens, I would encourage you to read with them about pornography addiction, study Scripture concerning sexual immorality, and keep an open dialogue about the subject in your home. Recent trends have demonstrated the issue of pornography is a growing problem among both boys and girls. Studies report that 93% of boys are exposed to internet porn before the age of 18. While that is shocking, they also found that 62% of girls reported exposure before the age of 18.[7] This is a problem for all young people today. Don't think the problem will only effect your sons. It may also be a problem for your daughters. To keep up with the latest issues regarding internet pornography, Just1ClickAway.org is a great resource from the Christian author and apologist Josh McDowell.

CULTIVATE STRONG RELATIONSHIPS WITH YOUR CHILDREN

Safeguards are great, but there is no replacement for a good relationship with your children. At a youth conference, I once heard Josh McDowell say, "Rules without relationship equals rebellion." I think he was spot on with that statement. It is important for parents to have well thought out rules in place. However, make sure to explain the rules as the guardrails of life. These guardrails keep us from going over the edge on sharp curves. They are there because of love not anger or hate. Encourage openness with your children. If your children come to you to admit a sin, and you act as if they just shot the president, you are creating children who fear confession. Cultivate an open relationship with your children.

One way you can do this is to confess your own shortcomings to them. You don't want your children having a false view of your holiness. Struggle is a part of everyone's sanctification. We do our best to battle with the flesh so we might walk in the Spirit (Gal. 5:16). When I fail as a parent, my wife, Amy, helps me see my blindspots and vice versa. If we do lose our temper or talk harshly with the kids, we point it out to each other in private. Let me emphasis the phrase *in private*. Even though one of us may have failed, we are still a team and have complete respect for one another. After the sin has been pointed out, the offender then confesses to our child and asks for forgiveness. Confessions between me and my child also happen in private. If one of them has something they need to confess to me that others do not need to be aware of, we talk through it together. I make sure he or she knows I have had and still have the same struggle at times. He or she routinely breathes a sigh of relief when they realize that their father could identify with their struggle. We hit our knees before God about private issues like this regularly.

When your child comes to you after making a poor choice, remember the *father* who runs to his child (Luke 15:20). You need to have a relationship with your children that allows them the ability to be honest about their struggles. One of my favorite verses is Proverbs 28:13: "He who conceals his transgressions will not prosper, but he who confesses and forsakes them will find compassion." Don't let your emotions in the moment lead your children to conceal their transgressions from you. Listen with understanding and be quick to restore and extend compassion.

Do you remember Jesus' parable of the Pharisee and the publican? It wasn't the well-disciplined Pharisee who was righteous before God. The one who was justified was the humbled publican. Our posture before God and others who confess sin needs to be like the tax collector, as seen in Luke 18:13-14:

> But the tax collector, standing some distance away, was even unwilling to lift up his eyes to heaven, but was beating his breast, saying, 'God, be merciful to me, the sinner!' I tell you, this man went to his house justified rather than the other; for everyone who exalts himself will be humbled, but he who humbles himself will be exalted.

You must set rules for your children concerning the usage of their devices. But, if they break a rule, have a relationship that seeks restoration. That doesn't mean you don't punish them. Just make sure that along with your rules comes relationship. Never forget, "While we were yet sinners, Christ died for us" (Rom. 5:6).

CHRISTIANS DON'T HAVE TO LOOK AT PORN

After actress Jennifer Lawrence's nude photo scandal made the headlines, she said something interesting. In a Vanity Fair article, Lawrence says, "I started to write an apology, but I don't have anything to say I'm sorry for… It was long distance, and either your boyfriend is going to look at porn, or he's going to look at you."[8] Notice the assumption that porn will be consumed if she doesn't send naked pictures of herself. Is this true for a born-again believer? Are we simply doomed without a real choice? Are we so crippled by the flesh that we cannot live by the Spirit? Not according to Paul. In Galatians 5:17-24, he indicates that we have a real choice when it comes to temptation:

> But I say, walk by the Spirit, and you will not carry out the desire of the flesh. For the flesh sets its desire against the Spirit, and the Spirit against the flesh; for these are in opposition to one another, so that you may not do the things that you please. But if you are led by the Spirit, you are not under the Law. Now the deeds of the flesh are evident, which are: immorality, impurity, sensuality, idolatry, sorcery, enmities, strife, jealousy, outbursts of anger, disputes, dissensions, factions, envying, drunkenness, carousing, and things like these, of which I forewarn you, just as I have forewarned you, that those who practice such things will not inherit the kingdom of God. But the fruit of the Spirit is love, joy, peace, patience, kindness, goodness, faithfulness, gentleness, self-control; against such things there is no law. Now those who belong to Christ Jesus have crucified the flesh with its passions and desires.

No Christian will be perfect until Christ returns and makes all things new. However, there should be a burning, Spirit-driven desire within us to put to death the deeds of the flesh. If you find out your child has been struggling with porn, you need to remind them that Christ is stronger than that problem. 1 John 4:4 says, "Greater is he who is in you than he who is in the world." We, along with our children, must make a concerted effort with the power of the Spirit to be thoughtful and practice righteousness.

A person doesn't become a great golfer overnight. A great golfer practices over and over and over again. He thinks about his every move. He agonizes over a weak spot in his game and works to strain it out. Christians must work at straining the sin out of our lives. We are not doomed to look at pornography and neither are our children. Paul makes it clear that we have the ability to walk by the Spirit and forego the desires of the flesh. Paul tells the Corinthian believers, "No temptation has overtaken you but such as is common to man; and God is faithful, who will not allow you to be tempted beyond what you are able, but with the temptation will provide the way of escape also, so that you will be able to endure it" (1 Cor. 10:13).

The temptations we deal with come from one of three places: the flesh, the world, or the devil. The first two we deal with on a daily basis. When two of these work in tandem, they are doubly strong — porn being the world and my flesh that may desire it. This is why our desires have to change, and we change by choosing to walk in the Spirit. We must beg God to help us not love the world. John explains this well in 1 John 2:15:

> Do not love the world nor the things in the world. If anyone loves the world, the love of the Father is not in him. For all that is in the world, the lust of the flesh and the lust of the eyes and the boastful pride of life, is not from the Father but is from the world.

Notice John says lust doesn't come from God. Lust is opposed to God and comes from the world. The Spirit is given from God (Acts 2). This is important for us to remember. We cannot blame our sin on God. James tells us God can't be tempted and doesn't tempt us (James 1:13). When you are dealing with that pull toward pornography (or any other sin), the world is tugging at your flesh. We must feed the Spirit not the flesh. What we feed becomes stronger. What we starve becomes weaker. You know this is true from experience. What are you feeding, and what are you starving in your life right now? What about your children? Are they feeding the flesh or the Spirit?

"For the mind set on the flesh is hostile toward God; for it does not subject itself to the law of God, for it is not even able to do so, and those who are in the flesh cannot please God" (Rom. 8:7). To stay in tune with the Holy Spirit, communicate with God through the disciplines and create a good accountability structure. Make sure you have these structures in place for your children as well. Protection apps are important, but nothing can replace open dialogue that allows for confession and repentance. Remember, the bearing of one another's burdens fulfills the law of Christ (Gal. 6:2).

I'M NOT HURTING ANYBODY

Many believe that looking at porn doesn't hurt anyone, so it's no big deal. Your teenage kids will hear this, so it's important for you to be able to combat it. The rationale says that because I am consuming it myself and no one else is involved, it can't really be that bad. This is false. God created sex for the union of marriage, and any sex celebrated outside of marriage is sinful. To watch others participating in sex for personal arousal is engaging in celebrating sexual activity outside the marriage relationship. Hebrews 13:4 says, "Marriage is to be held in honor among all, and the marriage bed is to be undefiled; for fornicators and adulterers God will judge."

It is also harmful for those practicing pornography. Their intimacy with one another is cheapened by receiving payment for the sexual act itself. Sex is a gift from one spouse to another. Also keep in mind there are people who do not participate in pornography willingly. Many are trapped in this situation and feel like there is no way out. Many are enslaved through human trafficking. The gospel is about liberation not slavery. Pornography degrades the souls of those who make it. They are made in the image of God and deserve more respect from us. Make sure and tell your children that many around the world are suffering right now as they participate in pornography.[9]

Pornography also hurts the consumer. It literally rewires a person's brain to want to consume more and more of it. Fightthenewdrug.org has incredible articles that explain the science surrounding porn addiction. Drug addicts crave a high from the drugs they consume because of the dopamine (a pleasure chemical) released in their brains. The more an addict uses their drug of choice, the more dopamine floods their brain, and the more pleasure is experienced. Porn works the same way. The more that is consumed, the more dopamine is poured into the human brain. This hurts the consumer! Porn is literally as addictive as a drug.[10] Drugs are not to be messed with. This is just a physical consequence of porn usage you can explain to your children. To take it a bit further, the guilt and shame that comes from consuming porn damages both the conscience and a person's relationship with the Lord.

Teach your children they are part of the body of Christ. Our decisions don't only reflect upon our own character, but they also reflect upon the body as a whole. When we act, we represent our church family and the Church universal, and these reflect upon Jesus Christ. Paul reminds us we are no longer to think of ourselves as autonomous agents, saying:

> ... do not go on presenting the members of your body to sin as instruments of unrighteousness; but present yourselves to God as those alive from the dead, and your members as instruments of righteousness to God. For sin shall not be master over you, for you are not under law but under grace.
> Romans 6:13-14

Our members (body parts) are to be used for God's glory. We are not autonomous, allowed to do anything we want. My father thought he wasn't hurting anyone with his pornography addiction when I was a kid. He never handed me his Playboy magazines to look at, but I found them. I'm sure he rationalized that his habit wasn't hurting anyone. What he didn't realize was that he hurt me.

Paul warns the Corinthian believers not to take part in sexual immorality. He urges them to flee from it and says, "Do you not know that your body is a temple of the Holy Spirit who is in you, whom you have from God, and that you are not your own? For you have been bought with a price: therefore glorify God in your body" (1 Cor. 6:19-20).

You can't say, "I'm not hurting anybody." You are not your own; you were bought with the precious blood of Jesus Christ! "Beloved, I urge you as aliens and strangers to abstain from fleshly lusts which wage war against the soul" (1 Pet. 2:11).

IDENTIFY YOUR WEAK TIMES AND BE ACCOUNTABLE

Have you stopped to reflect on when you are most vulnerable to committing sin with your eyes? Maybe it's when you are alone. Maybe it's when you're worn down and tired after a stressful day. We should work hard at identifying our triggers so our walk with Jesus stays strong. Talk with your children about identifying their triggers that lead to sin. Give them practical advice on how you protect yourself and how they can do the same. Again, a conversation that demonstrates both your feet of clay and your willingness to talk about the protections you place in your own life will open up conversations with your children. Being vulnerable with your children will help them in their weaknesses.

Remember, we are each part of the body of Christ. If you don't have a close fellow believer of the same gender to whom you can confess your weaknesses and ask for help, I want to encourage you to find that person — someone who will not just tell you everything is okay or that it's no big deal. Our desire for accountability and revealing our spiritual protection plans to our children will demonstrate that it's okay to be vulnerable, to confess, and that forgiveness from our Father is available. Modeling this and talking about it is way more powerful than simply giving directives to our children. We all need friends who are understanding and, at the same time, spur us on toward holiness. Help your children realize they not only have you but other Christian friends that can help keep them accountable in their weakness.

Questions to reflect on in this chapter:

1. Have I become desensitized to the overly sexualized culture I live in?
2. Do I know about my kid's daily internet activity? Am I as a parent in the dark?

3. Do I have the proper protections on my family's devices?
4. Am I diligently reading Scripture and other resources to help me and my children deal with sexual temptation?

Things to remember from this chapter:

1. The Nazis desensitized their recruits slowly over time. Culture does the same thing to us if we aren't vigilant.
2. Pornography moves through stages of addiction. Each level ramps up to a higher degree of exposure in order to receive the same high.
3. There is no one "good," no not one!
4. Cultivate strong relationships with your children where openness about sin is welcome. You don't want your kids to be afraid of confessing sin. You want them to desperately seek reconciliation through confession and repentance.
5. You and I as born-again believers have the ability to walk in the Spirit and not look at pornography.
6. You are a part of the body of Christ. You aren't only hurting yourself if you look at porn, but also your family and the Church.
7. Pornography also hurts the people who are involved in making the content. It damages their bodies and souls.
8. We shouldn't think everyone who is taking part in pornography is doing so willingly. Many are enslaved.
9. Accountability is critical when dealing with this issue. Find a friend who will be understanding and at the same time drive you toward holiness. Jesus didn't shed his blood for nothing. As John the Baptist said to the Pharisees, "show works worthy of repentance!"

CHAPTER NINE

COLLEGE: IS YOUR CHILD PREPARED?

Beloved, while I was making every effort to write you about our common salvation, I felt the necessity to write to you appealing that you contend earnestly for the faith which was once for all handed down to the saints.

Jude 3

"Modern culture is a mighty force. It is either subservient to the gospel or it is the deadliest enemy of the gospel. For making it subservient, religious emotion is not enough, intellectual labor is also necessary. And that labor is being neglected. The Church has turned to easier tasks. And now she is reaping the fruits of her indolence. Now she must battle for her life."[1]

J. Gresham Machen

I WASN'T PREPARED. ARE YOUR KIDS?

IN 1997, I WAS A NEW, ENTHUSIASTIC BELIEVER IN THE GOSPEL. I had been saved three years prior to my entering college and had become motivated to live out my faith. As new Christians, my friend and I were excited about the opportunity to take "The Old Testament as Literature" course to learn more about the Bible.

As the first class began, I quickly noticed that the professor's perspective completely differed from what I was being taught each Sunday at church. She started class with something like this, "As we talk about the Old Testament as literature, we must understand that nearly all countries in the world have a holy book. America for the most part has adopted the Bible as theirs. We know from science and observation that serpents don't talk, the seas don't part, and people most definitely don't rise from the dead. All these stories are written to challenge us to be better people. They aren't to be taken literally." I was stunned. I thought my friend and I were going to be learning the scriptures. Instead, the professor didn't believe the Bible had any real authority for life or practice, because in her eyes, the stories were mere fabrications.

I remember leaving class angry. I wasn't angry at the professor; I was angry at myself because I didn't know how to defend God's Word. I had either been lied to all my life at church, or this professor was lying. What was the truth?

I immediately went to a Christian bookstore and began searching the Christian Apologetics section. I found some great resources and even took one home, *A Ready Defense* by Josh McDowell. I consumed that book. I quickly learned that the professor's objections had already been answered by Christians, sometimes hundreds of years earlier. I also learned that my professor didn't actually know much of the Bible. During the course of the semester, my friend and I became friends with her. By the time the course neared its end, she would present the liberal position, then ask my friend and me to share our view with the class.

It was a great time of growth for me. I began to see that Scripture could be trusted. This experience prompted transfer to a Christian school and my major in biblical studies. I had originally observed many in the classroom losing faith in the Bible, but by the time class ended, I think young Christians in the room could see good reasons to believe the authority of Scripture.

What would happen to your child in that classroom? There are professors in secular colleges who would love nothing more than to crush your kids' faith in the gospel. The movie *God's Not Dead* typifies a college level classroom experience for students taking Philosophy 101. A Bible as literature class may actually be worse because many students who love the gospel, like myself, go in unsuspecting.

The believer must be prepared for battle. The apostle Paul paints the picture of a soldier preparing for battle in Ephesians 6:10-17. Verses 10-11 say, "Finally, be strong in the Lord and in the strength of his might. Put on the full armor of God, so that you will be able to stand firm against the schemes of the devil." In the temptation of Jesus, we see that the devil is a master at twisting language. He tries to bring confusion through misquoting Scripture (Matt. 4:6). I have seen many students leave church after their senior year strong in their faith only to return later skeptical of the scriptures. This happens not because Christianity isn't true, but because, like me, they go off to college unprepared, lacking the apologetics they will need when they get there.

If our Bible teaching at church and home never cracks the surface of David and Goliath and Jonah and the whale, our kids will not be prepared when they step into a college professor's class. The word *apologetics* comes from the Greek "apologia" and literally means "to make a defense."[2] When we make a defense of the truth, we throw words back at those purporting falsehood. Peter says, "But sanctify Christ as Lord in your hearts, always being ready to make a defense to everyone who asks you to give an account for the hope that is in you, yet with gentleness and reverence..." (1 Pet. 3:15).

I highly recommend parents read *Evidence That Demands a Verdict* by Josh and Sean McDowell with their teens. Josh McDowell has another great work called *Beyond Belief to Convictions*. Another helpful resource is *I Don't Have Enough Faith to be an Atheist* by Norm Geisler and Frank Turek. Also consider the book *Talking with Your Kids about God* by Natasha Crain. Read and discuss sections of these books with your children when they are juniors and seniors in high school. The content of these works provides great arguments not only for the existence of God but also for the validity of Scripture. Send copies of these books with your teen when they go off to college. If they are serious about their faith, they will not be shaken with these works nearby.

I also highly recommend sending your high school junior or senior to Summit Ministries for a twelve-day immersion in world-view training. This organization headed by Jeff Myers is for students sixteen to twenty-five years of age and has locations in California, Colorado, Pennsylvania, and Tennessee. I have sent several students to Summit Ministries, and they loved the experience. It's a great way to encourage and equip your kids to contend for the faith.

In this chapter, I will highlight some of what you should be prepared for and answer some common objections by skeptics. For more complete answers, I recommend consulting the suggested works dedicated to apologetics listed at the end of this chapter.

SCIENCE

Students are taught today in secular public institutions that evolution is an undisputed fact rather than a theory. Macroevolution is the idea of "monkey becoming man." This idea is not compatible with the scriptural record. Not only is it incompatible with Scripture but also with the fossil record. Many theistic evolutionists wax eloquent about the book of Genesis not being history. They claim it is a poetic work which tells an ancient allegory seeking to explain our current situation.

Anyone accepting this worldview and at the same time claiming to be a Christian runs into a profound problem — namely, the entire gospel hinges on the story of Adam and Eve. That isn't me talking; it's the Apostle Paul: "Therefore, just as through one man sin entered into the world, and death through sin, and so death spread to all men, because all sinned" (Rom. 5:12). If the story of Adam and Eve never actually happened, then how did sin enter the world? The book that narrates when the problem of sin originated also gives us the hope of the gospel. If we can't trust this book about the origin of the sin problem, then how can we trust it to tell us about God's solution through the coming Messiah?

The same chapter of Genesis that tells us about the origin of sin also prophesies the coming of Jesus. Genesis 3:15, given to us right after the curse from sin, is called the *protoevangelium* which means "the first good news."[3] The Bible tells us that "the seed of the woman will crush the head of the serpent" (Gen. 3:15). Since women don't have *seed*, we know this is speaking of a supernatural birth. Christ would be born through the virgin, Mary. If the story of Adam and Eve is mythical, then why is this promise not mythical? Is Genesis 3:15 mythical as well? Was Christ truly born of supernatural origins? We know the virgin birth idea was picked up after Genesis by the prophet Isaiah (Isa. 7:14). Later, both Matthew and Luke wrote that Jesus was the fulfillment of this promise (Matt. 1:18; Luke 1:34-35). The Genesis account is either historical, or it's not. Christians have good reason to hold their ground on the historicity of the text.

While some attack the historicity of Scripture subtly, others in the field of science attack it openly. Your kids should be ready for the straightforward attack on Christianity and for professors such as Richard Dawkins. In his book, *God Delusion*, he says, "The God of the Old Testament is arguably the most unpleasant character in all fiction: jealous and proud of it; a petty, unjust, unforgiving control-freak; a vindictive, bloodthirsty ethnic cleanser; a misogynistic, homophobic, racist, infanticidal, genocidal, filicidal, pestilential, megalomaniacal, sadomasochistic, capriciously malevolent bully."[4] When you read that, don't you just want to say, "Why don't you tell me what you really think?"

Stephen Meyer's two great works, *Signature in the Cell* and *Darwin's Doubt*, provide great arguments for reasons to doubt the belief in macroevolution. *Seven Days That Divide the World* by author and British Scientist John Lennox is another short and easy-to-understand work from the Christian perspective. You can also find debates online (these are sometimes easier to digest). Many persuasive agnostics and atheists today have major influence in our culture and on college campuses. The very eloquent astrophysicist Neil deGrasse Tyson has cast doubts in the minds of many as he frequently points out historical errors the Church made concerning Galileo and Copernicus.[5] While many of his critiques from church history are true, it doesn't necessarily follow that we should throw the baby out with the bathwater.

Parents used to fear their college-bound kids might feel pressured to engage in drinking or premarital sex. Those are still big concerns, but outright hostility toward Christianity is on the rise. Many professors see it as their job to mock the God of the Bible, leaving unequipped young people floundering in their chairs. Education itself has become so secularized that it is quite scary to consider what your kids will be exposed to. Make sure you equip them before they are faced with these hostilities.

PHILOSOPHY 101: YOUR KIDS NEED THEOLOGICAL GROUNDING AND RELATIONSHIPS

Philosophy means "love of wisdom."[6] Some philosophy professors believe it is their sole task to make your child lose their faith in God. "The unexamined life is not worth living," Socrates once wisely said.[7] "And this concept of God has not been carefully examined," the professor might quip. He might also say, "If God is all-loving, he can't be all powerful. If he is all-powerful, he can't be all loving. If he is all-loving, then he must not be all-powerful because he would take away all the evil in the world. If he is all-powerful, then he can't be all-loving because a loving God would never allow the atrocities we see to continue…" The professor might turn to your child and ask, "What about the people who have never heard about your Jesus? Are they doomed to eternal hell because they weren't born within the right zip code?"

I urge you to take this seriously. While these questions have been answered through the centuries many times and quite easily, kids leave the faith of their parents due to these arguments. The rate of the decline of faith in young people is alarming. We are failing to pass down faith that has conviction because we are passing down a faith with no substance. Because of this, we are losing our posterity to the world! Never say it couldn't happen to your kids. You must be diligent to equip them with good, solid philosophical and biblical arguments for these issues. *Is God a Moral Monster* by Paul Copan is one book which can help you equip your kids. It is a great apologetic work that answers many of the difficult Old Testament questions thoroughly.

In 2001, T.C. Pinckney told the Southern Baptist Convention Executive Committee in Nashville that Southern Baptists were losing 70-88% of their youth after their freshman year in college. Seventy percent of teenagers involved in church youth groups stop attending church within two years of their high school graduation.[8] This data was confirmed the next year when the SBC Family Life Council found that 88% of children in Evangelical homes leave church at the age of eighteen.[9]

Our David and Goliath and Samson and Delilah VBS stories aren't cutting it for the all-out assault coming at our kids in their first college philosophy class. They will face hard questions alone if they are not prepared. Questions like, "If God is loving what about the Old Testament Canaanite genocide? What about the Inquisition? The Crusades?" If we teach our children the answers to these questions and dig into a biblical philosophy with them, these questions won't phase them.

The Church at large has not prepared our kids for the spiritual war Paul warns is coming our way (Eph. 6). In *Soul Searching: The Religious and Spiritual Lives of American Teenagers*, Christian Smith and Melinda Lundquist Denton say their research shows most kids leave their faith because of skepticism.[10] Because they haven't been equipped, the college professor can easily tie them into knots in mere seconds. Campus Renewal, an organization that seeks to transform college campuses for Christ, says that in 2017 around 70% of kids coming from Christian homes were leaving the faith during their first year on a college campus.[11] Campus Renewal has established a "Campus Ministry Link" to support Christian kids by connecting them with other Christian students on the campus of their choosing.[12] Campus Renewal believes the Ministry Link is helpful because many students who become non-attenders during their first year of college do so only because they don't have relationships with other Christians. I highly recommend parents using The Campus Ministry Link with their children before they ever set foot on a secular campus away from home.

SEXUAL ETHICS

Founded in 1636, Harvard University was established with the chief end of bringing glory to Jesus Christ. In fact, its original mission statement clearly declared this purpose, "To be plainly instructed and consider well that the main end of your life and studies is to know God and Jesus Christ."[13] Later, because many believed Harvard was drifting from its original mission, a group of concerned Christians approached Elihu Yale. In 1718, he launched Yale University in order to bring a more conservative Christian approach to the university level. Yale's motto was not just *Veritas* "truth" like Harvard, but *Lux et Veritas*, meaning "light and truth."[14] Unfortunately, both of these universities once concerned with the glory of Christ and the spreading of the gospel are now the antithesis of their founding. Peter Greer of *Mission Drift* says:

> Our contention is not with the institutions Harvard and Yale are today. It's with the institutions they are not. Their founders were unmistakably clear in their goals: academic excellence and Christian formation. Today, they do something very different from their founding purpose. What happened to Harvard and Yale is the reality of Mission Drift.[15]

More recently we have seen Yale University spiral downward toward Sodom. Yale started "Sex Week" in 2002. A couple of students came up with the idea to dedicate a week to learning more about sex, not from a biblical point of view but from a totally secular worldview. Sex therapists, adult film stars, and persons of all sexual persuasions were hired to speak on various topics. Students learned about how to use sex toys, how to hook up "safely," and a myriad of other debaucheries during class time.[16] You may think you don't have to worry about things like Sex Week, but other universities have followed Yale's lead; Maryland, Harvard, Kentucky, Michigan, and many other universities have followed suit.

Christian kids have enough problems controlling the flesh with the help of the Holy Spirit, but something like this puts the young believer at even more risk, especially when it is so accepted not only by classmates but also by the professors. When speaking about the upcoming Sex Week at the University of Tennessee-Knoxville, best-selling author Todd Starnes said, "'Sex Week' — six days of XXX-rated debauchery that make Mardi Gras on Bourbon Street look like a Sunday school picnic."[17] This goes against Paul's encouragement in Philippians 4:8:

> Whatever is true, whatever is honorable, whatever is right, whatever is pure, whatever is lovely, whatever is of good repute, if there is any excellence and if anything worthy of praise, dwell on these things.

As believers, we must be very thoughtful about letting our children go headlong into spiritually hurtful situations. Even if they avoid Sex Week, they may take courses related to human sexuality that dismiss the biblical worldview as prudish and outdated. A close friend of mine has a teenage son who attends a Missouri junior college. His literature class required him to read a poem entitled "Three Oranges." I am not going to share the words of that poem in this book. You would be startled and alarmed that classrooms of young men and women are made to read such things aloud to one another. This is not education. It's perversion. It's slouching toward Sodom and Gomorrah, and it's unhealthy for Christian kids. If your children major in a field that requires classes on human sexuality, make sure they are equipped with a biblical worldview. You may also want to encourage them to ask about course content up front so they are not made to feel uncomfortable or bullied by their professors.

THE NEW TESTAMENT AS LITERATURE

I took a class titled "The New Testament as Literature" my sopho-more year in college. The professor told the class that the historicity of the person of Jesus was contested, and because of this, scholars had serious doubts about the accuracy in the transmission of the New Testament documents. These thoughts came from the authority in the room. College professors, in my mind, had to know what they were talking about. They were the experts, so I doubted the faith I had been handed down. The experience for me was much like that of my first Old Testament class. Until I began to research the claims, I wasn't for sure who to believe.

This worldview of Scripture being inaccurate and purely literary in its value is not an uncommon one. Author and editor of over thirty books, Bart D. Ehrman is a New Testament textual critic who serves as the professor of Religious Studies at the University of North Carolina Chapel Hill. He is famous for attempting to discredit the reliability of the New Testament in his books and debates. Ehrman points out the "discrepancies" in the resurrection accounts and the New Testament transmission variations, leading him to conclude that much if not most of the New Testament is not a reliable historical document. A quick YouTube search will yield many talks on this subject by Ehrman. It is not difficult to find scholars quick to contest Ehrman's assertions. When thinking through Ehrman's arguments, it is important to remember how the New Testament was transmitted to us. Until the invention of movable type with Guttenberg's press, a scribe was left to hand copy an ancient document. Former Professor of New Testament Language and Literature Bruce Metzger said of the ancient copyist process:

> One must bear in mind that the act of copying was in itself arduous and fatiguing, both because of the effort of sustained attention which it demanded as well as because of the cramped position of various muscles of the body. Though it seems strange to us today, in antiquity it was not customary to sit at a table or a

desk while writing. Both literary and artistic evidence suggests that until the early Middle Ages it was customary for scribes either to stand (while making relatively brief notes), or to sit on a stool or bench (or even on the ground), holding their scroll or codex on their knees. it goes without saying that such a posture was more tiring than sitting at a desk or writing table — though the latter must have been tiring enough to scribes thus occupied six hours a day month after month.[18]

There are currently over around 5,800 ancient Greek New Testament texts that have been discovered. No doubt, because of the difficulties in transmission that I just explained, there are some copyist errors that crept into the text. No one denies this. However, what Christians historically agree on is that the scriptures are inerrant and infallible in their original autographs. Don't let what I just said fool you. Although there are some errors in transmission (the copies), the New Testament's historical validity is like none other from the ancient world.

For one to argue that the New Testament is just another piece of literature is to ignore its unique transmission when compared to other famous ancient works of literature. Some of the 5,800 Greek New Testament manuscripts are just portions or fragments of a letter of Paul or a gospel. But when all the manuscripts are taken together and translated, it is clear that God kept the authors from theological error. In fact, the text we have today is nearly 99% accurate grammatically and 100% accurate theologically. No other book in antiquity has that volume of transmission copies. This not only shows how the spread of the Christian message was impacting many societies but also how God supernaturally preserved the message to be handed down for Christians in future ages. Again, no other work has been transmitted so meticulously and carefully in antiquity. The charts below demonstrate the reliability of the New Testament when compared to other ancient works.[19]

AUTHOR	BOOK	DATE WRITTEN	EARLIEST COPIES	TIME GAP	# OF COPIES
Homer	Iliad	800 B.C.	400 B.C.	400 years	643
Herodotus	History	480-425 B.C.	A.D. 900	1,350 years	8
Thucydides	History	460-400 B.C.	A.D. 900	1,300 years	8
Plato		400 B.C.	A.D. 900	1,300 years	7
Demosthenes		300 B.C.	A.D. 1100	1,400 years	200
Caesar	Gallic Wars	100-44 B.C.	A.D. 900	1,000 years	10
Livy	Hist. of Rome	59 B.C.-A.D. 17	10 century	1000 years	19 copies
Tacitus	Annals	A.D. 100	A.D. 1100	1,000 years	20
Pliny Secundus	Natural History	AD 61-113	A.D. 850	750 years	7
John	N.T.	A.D. 50-100	A.D. 120	50 years	Fragments

The Rest of the New Testament

AUTHOR	BOOK	DATE WRITTEN	EARLIEST COPIES	TIME GAP	NUMBER OF COPIES
THE REST OF THE NEW TESTAMENT			A.D. 200 BOOKS OF NEW TESTAMENT	100 YEARS	
THE REST OF THE NEW TESTAMENT			A.D. 250 MOST OF NEW TESTAMENT	150 YEARS	
THE REST OF THE NEW TESTAMENT			A.D. 325 COMPLETE NEW TESTAMENT	225 YEARS	5,600 GREEK MANUSCRIPTS
THE REST OF THE NEW TESTAMENT			A.D. 400-500 (OTHER TRANSLATIONS)	400 YEARS	19,000 MANUSCRIPTS

Not only do we have the above reasons to believe in the historical reliability of Scripture, but we also have outside historical sources that advocate for the story of Scripture as a whole. Many historians in modern education try to deny historical claims of Christianity. They speak as if Jesus' followers made up the major tenets of Christianity, thus neither the New Testament nor its claims can be trusted. New Testament scholar and philosopher Gary Habermas developed years ago what he called the "minimal facts argument" regarding the resurrection of Jesus. Here is how it works. Habermas consulted scholarship outside of the New Testament to prove his case. He scanned accepted historical literature from the first couple centuries AD. He went to non-religious, atheist, and agnostic sources. It didn't matter as long as the source was not biblical. He consulted these outside sources for early testimony about Jesus. Habermas concluded six minimal facts from early non-believers.[20] These compelling facts include the following:

1. That Jesus died by crucifixion
2. That very soon afterwards, his followers had real experiences that they thought were actual appearances of the risen Jesus
3. That their lives were transformed as a result, even to the point of being willing to die specifically for their faith in the resurrection message
4. That these things were taught very early, soon after the crucifixion
5. That James, Jesus' unbelieving brother, became a Christian due to his own experience that he thought was the resurrected Christ
6. That the Christian persecutor Paul (formerly Saul of Tarsus) also became a believer after a similar experience.[21]

Historians who bash Christianity because of the evils done in its name need to read the words of Jesus. Historians who try to claim the major tenets of Christianity are fabricated need to be honest about the first and second century sources outside of the New Testament that corroborate its claims.

HISTORICAL SOURCES (NON-CHRISTIAN)

What do the following persons and book have in common: Josephus, Tacitus, Pliny, Thallus, Suetonius, Phlegon, Lucian, Celsus, Mara Bar-Serapion, and The Jewish Talmud? None were of Christian influence. These men all lived within the first two centuries of the Church, and The Talmud was written during that time as well. In the writings of these unbelievers, we can observe the following picture of Jesus:

1. Jesus lived during the time of Tiberius Caesar.
2. He lived a virtuous life.
3. He was a wonder-worker.
4. He had a brother named James.
5. He was acclaimed to be the Messiah.
6. He was crucified under Pontius Pilate.
7. He was crucified on the eve of the Jewish Passover.
8. Darkness and an earthquake occurred when he died.
9. His disciples believed he rose from the dead.
10. His disciples were willing to die for their belief.
11. Christianity spread rapidly as far as Rome.
12. His disciples denied the Roman gods and worshiped Jesus as God.[22]

This information from unbelievers should prove beyond doubt that Jesus was a real human being. I don't have time to quote all these writers, but here is one truly amazing admission about Jesus by Jewish historian Josephus who wrote prolifically during the first century. In his *Antiquities of the Jews*, an extensive quote mentions Christ. Although many have claimed it is an interpolation (added later by Christians), every single copy of his work ever discovered included this passage.[23] Book 18 of the collection, chapter 3 reads:

> About this time there lived Jesus, a wise man if indeed one ought
> to call him a man. For he was one who wrought surprising feats
> and was a teacher of such people as accept the truth gladly. He

won over many Jews and many of the Greeks. He was the Christ. When Pilate, upon hearing him accused by men of the highest standing amongst us, had condemned him to be crucified, those who had in the first place come to love him did not give up their affection for him. On the third day he appeared to them restored to life, for the prophets of God had prophesied these and countless other marvelous things about him. And the tribe of the Christians, so called after him, has still to this day not disappeared.[24]

Josephus lived during the first century and could have written this around AD 93 or 94. This is pretty compelling evidence not only of Jesus' existence but also to the details of the beliefs of his early followers. Josephus wrote extensively during the first century and his knowledge of first century events can be clearly recognized by reading his works. Your kids need to know that within sixty years of the Christ's ascension, these were the things being circulated about Jesus from the Middle East all the way to Rome (where Josephus was writing).[25] The picture of Jesus we get from these historians can easily be found in other works dedicated to apologetics or even with a simple online search.

HISTORICAL SOURCES (CHRISTIAN)

Apologist J. Warner Wallace says that, from a careful reading of the early church fathers, it is possible to construct a theology of Jesus that perfectly matches what we see in the New Testament. Wallace says:

The early church fathers did confirm enough of the New Testament claims to validate and authenticate the writings of the apostles. From the non-canonical works of Ignatius and Polycarp (students of John) and the non-canonical work of Clement (a student of Paul) we can determine the following:

1. Jesus was predicted by the Old Testament as described in the New Testament.
2. Jesus is divine as described in the New Testament.

3. Jesus taught his disciples as described in the New Testament.
4. Jesus worked miracles as described in the New Testament.
5. Jesus was born of a virgin as described in the New Testament.
6. Jesus lived, ministered, was crucified, and died as described in the New Testament.
7. Jesus rose from the dead and demonstrated his deity as described in the New Testament.[26]

That list of six truths is the bedrock of the early church. We can see that not only is the manuscript evidence abundant but its consistency with the testimony of the early church fathers is a fact. The early church fathers listed by Wallace were disciples of the disciples. This then is clear, compelling evidence that the New Testament story can be trusted. The message of the Bible from the earliest times forward is superior in every way to other literature of antiquity.

ARGUMENTS AGAINST CHRISTIANITY IN HISTORY

Many grievous errors have been and continue to be committed by people claiming to be Christians. Whether they are believers or not, God will judge. We must remember, however, that all who march under the banner of Christ do not necessarily speak for the founder. As Europeans followed the call of Pope Urban II to fight the Muslims in AD 1096, the crusading armies in route to Jerusalem slaughtered many Jews, including children, across German cities. The crusaders' rationale? The Jews' ancestors had murdered Jesus, and they were believed to be enemies of the gospel.[27] However, the fact that this happened doesn't mean Christianity is bad. It means the people who committed the crimes were bad.

When evaluating the activity of a person claiming to be a Christian, we must define what "Christian" means. If we say we are a Christ follower, we must then walk as Jesus walked. Does Jesus condone crusaders slaughtering innocent Jews across Europe because they are "the enemies of Christ?" Absolutely not! Don't blame Christianity for what some claiming to be Christ followers did. The founder defines the religion, and on the question of whether or not it's okay to kill Jews, our founder is clear. Even if the Jews were the enemy of Christians (which they are not), we are commanded by our founder to "love our enemies" (Matt 5:44). Consider the following Scripture recorded in Jesus' most famous sermon, the Sermon on the Mount, and apply it across the board to the Crusades, the Inquisition, the Salem Witch trials, and any other number of sketchy historical problems:

> You have heard that it was said, 'you shall love your and hate your enemy.' But I say to you, love your enemies and pray for those who persecute you, so that you may be sons of your Father who is in heaven; for he causes his sun to rise on the evil and the good, and sends rain on the righteous and the unrighteous. For if you love those who love you, what reward do you have? Do not even the tax collectors do the same? If you greet only your brothers, what more are you doing than others? Do not even the Gentiles do the same? Therefore you are to be perfect, as your heavenly Father is perfect.
> Matthew 5:43-48

This is how our founder viewed his fellow man. Dying as an innocent man on a cross, he uttered these as some of his last words, "Father forgive them; they know not what they do" (Luke 23:34). The issue is with imperfect followers and people who use the name of Christ but are not really followers. Jesus defines our religion, but don't think he is weak. They murdered him for his claims not because he went along with popular opinion. While we may grant that many false and grievous things have been done in the name of Christ, it is unfair to apply that to Jesus or those who belong to the true Church who labor to spread the love of the gospel.

Questions to reflect on in this chapter:

1. Are my children prepared to face the onslaught of criticism toward the Bible that college sometimes brings?
2. Will I take steps to prepare my children in some basic apologetics so they can trust Scripture?
3. Will I take the time to read a good Christian book like *Beyond Belief to Convictions* with my children so they know the scriptures are trustworthy?
4. Am I willing to always parent my children? When they get old enough to leave the house, will I lovingly continue to nurture and guide them?

Things to remember from this chapter:

1. Good answers to defend the Christian faith are out there. We are a people with a rich history and tradition of truth.
2. There are great organizations like Summit Ministries to help equip kids for the worldview they will encounter in college.
3. If monkey to man (macroevolution) is true, then the Genesis account of how sin and death entered the world cannot be trusted. We must trust Scripture and know the arguments against macroevolution.
4. Scripture is trustworthy based on manuscript evidence, and it's corroborated by the writings of the early church fathers.
5. Don't blame the founder for the errors committed by others in history. Let the founder define the religion.

Apologetic resources that can help you combat some questions your kids may have during their college years:

— *Christian Apologetics* (Douglas Groothuis)
— *The Case for Christ* (Lee Strobel)

— *The New Evidence that Demands a Verdict* (Josh and Sean McDowell)
— *The Apologist's Tool Kit* (Rob Phillips)
— *I Don't Have Enough Faith to be an Atheist* (Norm Geisler, Frank Turek)
— *Talking with Your Kids About God* (Natasha Crain)
— *Are the New Testament Documents Reliable* (F.F. Bruce)
— *Cold-Case Christianity* (J. Warner Wallace)
— *Seven Days that Divide the World* (John Lennox)
— *The Battle for the Beginning: Creation, Evolution and the Bible* (John MacArthur)
— *Is God a Moral Monster* (Paul Copan)
— *Letter from a Christian Citizen* (Doug Wilson) This is an answer to Sam Harris' book, *Letter to a Christian Nation*.
— I also highly recommend watching the documentary *Collision* which includes a series of debates between famous atheist Christopher Hitchens and Pastor Douglas Wilson.

FINAL THOUGHTS

AS PARENTS, OUR GOAL SHOULD NOT BE TO RAISE OUR KIDS AS quickly as possible so we can move on with our lives. Our goal should be a lifelong commitment to spiritually building up our children so they are prepared not only for this life but also for the life to come. In order to do this, we will have to make some tough decisions along the way. 1 Corinthians 15:33 says, "Bad company corrupts good morals." Sometimes our children will get mad at us for not letting them hang out with certain people. Sometimes they won't understand because they just aren't old enough to "get it." Sometimes they may even be mocked or made fun of by "friends" because you have had to take a hard stand on something, such as not letting them have a cell phone (if that's your stance). All of this is, of course, a part of faithful parenting.

This book began with talking about building the gospel into your young children. It ends with a call to equip your college-aged children. But don't think you are done. I want to acknowledge how grateful I am that my parents haven't stopped "parenting" me. At forty-two, I can see how my simplistic, teenage thinking would have gotten me into a lot more trouble had it not been for them. I still learn from them. I have asked for forgiveness more than once for being a stubborn kid who had to learn the hard way. My mother and stepfather aren't perfect people, but they loved the gospel and always pointed me to Jesus. For that, I am eternally grateful. If you do the same, I am confident your children will one day say the same thing about you.

> Peter said to them, 'Repent, and each of you be baptized in the name of Jesus Christ for the forgiveness of your sins; and you will receive the gift of the Holy Spirit. For the promise is for you and your children and for all who are far off, as many as the Lord our God will call to himself.'
>
> Acts 2:38-39

May God bless your families for generations to come.

NOTES

CHAPTER ONE

1. Thabiti M. Anyabwile, *What is a Healthy Church Member* (Wheaton, IL: Crossway Books, 2008), 39.
2. C.S. Lewis, *Mere Christianity* (New York: HarperCollins, 1952/2001), 56.
3. Augustine, *The Confessions of St. Augustine*, translated by Rex Warner (New York: The New York American Library), Book 8, Ch. 7, pg. 174.
4. John Calvin, "Acts of the Council of Trent with the Antidote," accessed May 2019, http://www.monergism.com/thethreshold/sdg/calvin_trentantidote.html.
5. J. Ramsey Michaels, *I Peter*, World Biblical Commentary (Nashville, TN: Nelson Reference & Electronic, 1988), 268
6. Richard N. Longenecker, *Acts*, The Expositor's Bible Commentary (Grand Rapids, MI: Zondervan Publishing House, 1981), 402
7. Walter Bauer, Fredrick Danker, *Greek-English Lexicon of the New Testament and other Early Christian Literature*, 3rd ed. (Chicago, IL: The University of Chicago Press, 2000), 609
8. Matt Slick, "How many times do various words appear in the Bible," accessed May 2019, https://carm.org/how-many-times-do-various-words-appear-in-the-bible.
9. Nathan W. Bingham, "What Does 'Simul Justus et Peccator' Mean," Ligonier Ministries, published October 16, 2018, https://www.ligonier.org/blog/simul-justus-et-peccator/.
10. Lyrics, Edward Mote, 1834. Composer, William B. Bradbury, 1863. *My Hope is Built on Nothing Less*.
11. "Preamble Confessional Statement: Theological Vision for Ministry," Article 8: The Justification of Sinners, The Gospel Coalition, accessed May 2019, https://www.thegospelcoalition.org/about/foundation-documents/#confessional-statement.
12. "1689 Baptist Confession Chapter 13," Association of Reformed Baptist Churches of America, accessed May 2019, http://www.arbca.com/1689-chapter13.
13. R.C. Sproul, *Chosen by God* (Carol Stream, IL: Tyndale House Publishers, 1986), 66.
14. Thomas Watson, *The Doctrine of Repentance* (Carlisle, PA: The Banner of Truth Trust, 1987), 18.
15. Walter Bauer, Fredrick Danker, *Greek-English Lexicon of the New Testament and other Early Christian Literature*, 640.
16. Thomas Watson, *The Doctrine of Repentance, 18.*
17. Thomas K. Ascol, *Truth and Grace Memory Book 1* (Cape Coral, FL: Founders Press, 2017), 41-42.

CHAPTER TWO

1. Eric T. Eichinger, *The Final Race*, (Carol Stream, IL: Tyndale House Publishers, 2018).
2. Douglas Wilson, *The Paideia of God: And Other Essays on Education*, (Moscow, ID: Cannon Press, 1999), 9-10.
3. Wilson, *The Paideia of God: And Other Essays on Education*, 10.
4. Wilson, *The Paideia of God: And Other Essays on Education*, 11.
5. *Plastic Surgery Statistics Report*, PDF. American Society of Plastic Surgeons, 2016.
6. Sky Gould, Dave Mosher, "Americans Spent 8 Billion on Plastic Surgery in 2016," May 22, 2017, https://www.businessinsider.com/plastic-surgery-growth-statistics-facts-2016-2017-5.
7. Francis Brown, S.R. Driver, C.A. Briggs, *Hebrew and English Lexicon of the Old Testament*, (Oxford, England: Clarendon Press, 1906), 315.
8. Joi-Marie McKenzie, "David Cassidy's Daughter Reveals His Final Words," ABC News, November 25, 2017, https://abcnews.go.com/Entertainment/david-cassidys-daughter-reveals-final-words/story?id=51377243.
9. Dr. R. Albert Mohler Jr., "'God Made Me for China' — Eric Liddell Beyond Olympic Glory," Albert Mohler, July 25, 2017, https://albertmohler.com/2017/07/25/god-made-china-eric-liddell-beyond-olympic-glory/.
10. Mohler Jr., "'God Made Me for China' — Eric Liddell Beyond Olympic Glory."
11. Eric Metaxas, *7 Men* (Nashville, TN: Nelson Books, 2013), 71.
12. Mohler Jr., "'God Made Me for China' — Eric Liddell Beyond Olympic Glory."
13. Metaxas, *7 Men*, 67.
14. Metaxas, 71.
15. Metaxas, 86.
16. Sally Magnusson, *The Flying Scotsman, A Biography* (New York, NY: Quartet Books Inc., 1981), 160-170.

CHAPTER THREE

1. Stephen J. Nichols, *The Reformation: How a Monk and a Mallet Changed the World*. (Wheaton, IL: Crossway Books, 2007), 37.
2. Ken Curtis, Ph.D., *Martin Luther: Monumental Reformer*, Christianity.com, April 28, 2010, https://www.christianity.com/church/church-history/timeline/1501-1600/martin-luther-monumental-reformer-11629922.html.
3. Stephen J. Nichols, *The Reformation: How a Monk and a Mallet Changed the World*, 31.
4. Brian Lisi, "Pastor Whose Wife was Murdered..." Daily News, April 25, 2016, https://www.nydailynews.com/news/crime/pastor-wife-murdered-year-forgives-kil-article-1.2613889.
5. Rebecca Barnes, "The Rest of the Story," Christianity Today, January 1, 2006, https://www.christianitytoday.com/ct/2006/january/30.38.html.
6. Justin Taylor, "He Was No Fool," The Gospel Coalition, January 9, 2010, https://www.thegospelcoalition.org/blogs/justin-taylor/he-ws-no-fool/.
7. Gorden J. Wenham, *Word Biblical Commentary: Genesis 1-15*. (Waco, TX: Word Books, 1987), 68.

CHAPTER FOUR

1. Donald S. Whitney, *Spiritual Disciplines for the Christian Life*, (Carol Stream, IL: Nav Press, 1991), 112.
2. Dr. Kara E. Powell, Dr. Chap Clark, *Sticky Faith* (Grand Rapids, MI: Zondervan, 2011), 35.
3. Dallas Willard, *The Spirit of the Disciplines*, (New York, NY: HarperCollins, 1988), xii.
4. Dallas Willard, *The Spirit of the Disciplines*.
5. Raymond Edman, *The Disciplines of Life*, (Wheaton, IL: Van Kampen Press, 1948).
6. Greg Ogden, *Discipleship Essentials* (Downers Grove, IL: Intervarsity Press, 1998), 46.
7. R.A. Torrey, *How to Pray* (New Kensington, PA: Whitaker House, 1983), 56.
8. *Eusebius: The Church History*, trans. Paul L. Maier (Grand Rapids, MI: Kregel Publications, 1999), 81.
9. Dick Eastman, *The Hour that Changes the World* (Fairfax, VA: Chosen Books, 2002), 21.
10. St. Augustine, *Confessions Book 8* (Nashville, TN: Thomas Nelson Publishers, 1999), 171.
11. Howard and Mrs. Taylor, *Hudson Taylor in Early Years: The Growth of a Soul* (Overseas Missionary Fellowship, 1989).
12. D.A. Carson, *Memoirs of an Ordinary Pastor: The Life and Reflections of Tom Carson* (Wheaton, IL: Crossway Books, 2008), 72.
13. John MacArthur, *The MacArthur New Testament Commentary: II Timothy* (Chicago, IL: Moody Press, 1995), 142-143.
14. John Foxe, *Foxe's Book of Martyrs* (Peabody, MA: Hendrickson Christian Classics, 2004), 232.
15. John Foxe, *Foxe's Book of Martyrs*, 230.
16. Bruce L. Shelley, *Church History in Plain Language*, 3rd Ed. (Nashville, TN: Thomas Nelson Publishing, 2008), 265.
17. Shelley, *Church History in Plain Language*, 266.
18. Shelley, *Church History in Plain Language*, 267.
19. Shelley, *Church History in Plain Language*, 266.
20. Shelley, *Church History in Plain Language*, 268.
21. Shelley, *Church History in Plain Language*, 269.
22. *State of the Church and Family Report*, online excerpt, Barna Group, 2016, https://www.barna.com/research/state-church-2016/.
23. *State of the Church and Family Report*, online excerpt, Barna Group, 2016, https://www.barna.com/research/state-church-2016/.

CHAPTER FIVE

1. Charles Spurgeon, "A Pastoral Visit," Sermon, Metropolitan Tabernacle, London, England, 1908.
2. "Shorter Catechism," The Orthodox Presbyterian Church, accessed May 2019, https://www.opc.org/sc.html.
3. St. Augustine, *Confessions Book 1* (Nashville, TN: Thomas Nelson Publishers, 1999), 17.

4. Edgar Albert Guest, "It Couldn't Be Done," Poetry Foundation, accessed May 2019, www.poetryfoundation.org/poems/44314/it-couldnt-be-done.
5. Rick Warren, Facebook Post, posted April 3, 2012, accessed May 2019, https://www.facebook.com/pastorrickwarren/posts/10150780131955903.
6. Spurgeon, "A Pastoral Visit."
7. Thomas K. Ascol, *Truth and Grace Memory Book 1* (Cape Coral, FL: Founders Press, 2017), 23-24.
8. B.K. Kuiper, *The Church in History* (Grand Rapids, MI: W.M.B. Eerdmans Publishing, 1951), 163.

CHAPTER SIX

1. Andy Crouch, *The Tech-Wise Family* (Grand Rapids, MI: BakerBooks, 2017), 168.
2. Nancy Pearcy, "Silicon Valley's Drug Fueled Secret Sex Parties—One More Reason to Hate the Hookup Culture," Fox News, January 6, 2018, http://www.foxnews.com/opinion/2018/01/06/silicon-valleys-drug-fueled-secret-sex-parties-one-more-reason-to-hate-hookup-culture.html
3. Corrie Ten Boom, *The Hiding Place* (New York, NY: Bantam Books, 1984), 26-27.
4. Christopher Yuan, *Holy Sexuality and the Gospel* (New York, NY: Multnomah, 2018), 99.
5. Iain H. Murray, *Amy Carmichael: Beauty for Ashes* (Edinburgh, UK: The Banner of Truth Trust, 2015).
6. Dave and Neta Jackson, *Hero Tales*, Vol. 3 (Minneapolis, MN: Bethany House Publishers, 1998), 119-121.

CHAPTER SEVEN

1. Charles Spurgeon, *Morning and Evening* (Grand Rapids, MI: Discovery House, 2016), 205.
2. Kathy Schiffer, "When Mozart Disobeyed the Pope," National Catholic Register, August 19, 2016, http://www.ncregister.com/blog/kschiffer/when-mozart-disobeyed-the-pope.
3. Brian and Louise Hogan, "History of Mission," The Traveling Team, http://www.thetravelingteam.org/articles/brian-louise-hogan.
4. D.A. Carson, *Expositor's Bible Commentary* (Grand Rapids, MI: Zondervan Publishing House, 1984), 393.
5. Ralph D. Winter, *The Three Mission Eras*, PDF, World Evangelicals, 268, http://www.worldevangelicals.org/resources/rfiles/res3_426_link_1342021359.pdf.
6. David M. Howard, "Student Power in World Missions," In *Perspectives on the World Christian Movement*, edited by Ralph D. Winter and Steven C. Hawthorne, 4th ed, (Pasadena, CA: William Carey Library, 2009), 307.
7. David M. Howard, "Student Power in World Missions," 307.

CHAPTER EIGHT

1. Josh McDowell, Just 1 Click Away, accessed May 2019, https://www.josh.org/category/relationships/sex-pornography/.
2. Dr. James Dobson, *Bringing Up Boys* (Wheaton, IL: Tyndale House Publishers, 2001), 213.
3. Dr. James Dobson, *Bringing Up Boys*, 213.
4. Alex .A, "'Pandora's Box was Actually 'Pandora's Jar,'" The Vintage News, September 16, 2016, https://www.thevintagenews.com/2016/09/16/pandoras-box-actually-pandoras-jar-translation-error-made-500-years-ago-persisted-day/.
5. *The Porn Phenomenon: The Impact of Pornography in the Digital Age*, PDF, Barna Group in Partnership with Josh McDowell Minsitry, 2016, 28-29, https://www.cbcrh.com/home/180005292/180009741/docs/The-Porn-Phenomenon.pdf?sec_id=180009741.
6. Andy Crouch, *The Tech-Wise Family* (Grand Rapids, MI: Baker Books, 2017), 175.
7. *Porn Stats*, PDF, Covenant Eyes, 2015, 15, https://www.bevillandassociates.com/wp-content/uploads/2015/05/2015-porn-stats-covenant-eyes-1.pdf.
8. Sam Kashner. Both Huntress and Prey. (Vanity Fair: November 2014). https://www.vanityfair.com/hollywood/2014/10/jennifer-lawrence-photo-hacking-privacy
9. Abigail Biggs, Pornography and Crime. July 21st 2016. Just1clickaway.org. https://www.josh.org/pornography-and-crime/
10. "How Porn Affects the Brain Like a Drug," Fight the New Drug, August 23, 2017, https://fightthenewdrug.org/how-porn-affects-the-brain-like-a-drug/

CHAPTER NINE

1. J. Gresham Machen, "Christianity and Culture," *The Princeton Theological Review* 11, no. 1 (1913): 13, accessed May 2019.
2. Rob Philips, *The Apologetics Toolkit*, 3rd ed. (Jefferson City, MO: Missouri Baptist Convention, 2016), 12.
3. Victor P. Hamilton, *Handbook on the Pentateuch*, 2nd ed. (Grand Rapids, MI: Baker Academic, 2005), 44.
4. Richard Dawkins, *The God Delusion* (New York, NY: Houghton Mifflin Company, 2006), 31.
5. Fr. Robert J. Spitzer, "A Catholic Response to Neil deGrasse Tyson's Cosmos," Magis Center, 2018, accessed May 2019, https://www.magiscenter.com/a-catholic-response-to-neil-degrasse-tysons-cosmos-filling-in-the-intellectual-gaps/.
6. Ed L. Miller, *Questions That Matter: An Invitation to Philosophy*, 4th ed. (New York, NY: McGraw Hill, 1996), 3.
7. Britt-Marie Schiller, Ph.D., "Perspectives: The Unexamined Life Is Not Worth Living," Saint Louis Psychoanalytic Institute, accessed May 2019, https://www.stlpi.org/perspectives-the-unexamined-life-is-not-worth-living/.
8. T.C. Pinckney, "We are Losing Our Children," Alliance for the Separation of School and State, September 18, 2001, http://www.schoolandstate.org/SBC/Pinckney-WeAreLosingOurChildren.htm
9. Jon Walker, "Family Life Council Says It's Time to Bring Family Back to Life,"

The Highest Power for the Greatest Task, June 12, 2002, http://www.sbcannualmeeting.net/sbc02/newsroom/newspage.asp?ID=261.

10. Christian Smith, Melinda Lundquist Denton, *Soul Searching: The Religious and Spiritual Lives of American Teenagers* (New York, NY: Oxford University Press, 2009), 89.

11. Michael F. Haverluck, "Ministries Tackle 70% Rate of College Students Leaving Faith," One News Now, August 13, 2017, https://onenewsnow.com/church/2017/08/13/ministries-tackle-70-rate-of-college-students-leaving-faith.

12. Campus Ministry Link, accessed May 2019, https://campusministrylink.org/vision/.

13. Peter Greer, Chris Horst, *Mission Drift* (Bloomington, MN: Bethany House Publishers, 2014), 18.

14. Peter Greer, Chris Horst, *Mission Drift*, 19.

15. Peter Greer, Chris Horst, *Mission Drift*, 18.

16. Bijan Aboutorabi, "What You Can Learn from 'Sex Week' at Yale," Intercollegiate Studies Institute, June 24, 2015, https://home.isi.org/what-you-can-learn-sex-week-yale.

17. Todd Starnes, "University's 'Sex Week' Sounds Like a Porn Film Title—But Unbelievably, It's Real," Fox News, April 5, 2018, https://www.foxnews.com/opinion/todd-starnes-universitys-sex-week-sounds-like-a-porn-film-title-but-unbelievably-its-real

18. Bruce M. Metzger, *The Text of the New Testament: It's Transmission, Corruption and Restoration* (Oxford, UK: Oxford University Press, 1992.), 16-17.

19. Josh McDowell, *Beyond Belief to Convictions* (Wheaton, IL: Tyndale House Publishers, 2002), 174-175.

20. Gary Habermas, "Minimal Facts on the Resurrection that Even Skeptics Accept," Southern Evangelical Seminary and Bible College, accessed May 2019, https://ses.edu/minimal-facts-on-the-resurrection-that-even-skeptics-accept/.

21. Gary Habermas, "Minimal Facts…"

22. Norm Geisler, Frank Turek, *I Don't Have Enough Faith to be an Atheist* (Wheaton, IL: Crossway Books, 2004), 221-223.

23. Kyle Butt M.Div., "The Historical Christ—Fact or Fiction?" Apologetics Press, 2000, https://www.apologeticspress.org/apcontent.aspx?category=10&article=187.

24. Flavius Josephus, *The Works of Josephus: Antiquities of the Jews* (Peabody, MA: Hendrickson Publishers, 1980), 480.

25. Kyle Butt M.Div., "The Historical Christ—Fact or Fiction?"

26. J. Warner Wallace, "Can We Construct the Entire New Testament from the Writings of the Church Fathers?" Cold-Case Christianity, June 13, 2016, http://coldcasechristianity.com/2016/can-we-construct-the-entire-new-testament-from-the-writings-of-the-church-fathers/.

27. Thomas F. Madden, *The Concise History of the Crusades* (Lanham, MD: Rowman & Littlefield Publishers, 1999), 20-21.

ACKNOWLEDGMENTS

There are many people to thank for their support on this project. My wife, Amy, has encouraged me from the idea phase of this book all the way through to the finished product. She has read many iterations of each chapter and made lots of helpful suggestions along the way. I also want to thank Brianna Boes for her hard work in the editing process and layout of this book. Her thoughtful questions challenged me and helped me tighten up my arguments. I want to thank Sarah Benz for her outstanding work on designing the cover. I also want to thank my biological parents and step-parents for pouring into my life and loving me unconditionally.

ALSO BY MARTIN WINSLOW

NEW TESTAMENT 260: A ONE-YEAR NEW TESTAMENT READING PLAN AND NAVIGATIONAL TOOL

This is a one year New Testament bible reading program. Take away weekends and you have 260 days in a solar year. This is the exact number of New Testament chapters! Read through the New Testament and learn a paraphrase (an important fact) from every single chapter! When memorized it helps a person navigate the New Testament with fluidity. Also, learn a key verse for every week, along with a fun fact and prayer for the week. Musical downloads containing the paraphrases in each New Testament book are sold separately on the website www.nextgenerationfaithfulness.com

Available on Amazon and at Next Generation Faithfulness:

Blog: www.nextgenerationfaithfulness.com

Made in the USA
Columbia, SC
05 August 2019